Rape in Early Modern England

Helen Barker

Rape in Early Modern England

Law, History and Criticism

palgrave
macmillan

Helen Barker
London, UK

ISBN 978-3-030-82608-6 ISBN 978-3-030-82609-3 (eBook)
https://doi.org/10.1007/978-3-030-82609-3

This Palgrave Macmillan imprint is published by the registered company Springer Nature Switzerland AG.
The registered company address is: Gewerbestrasse 11, 6330 Cham, Switzerland

For LKB

Preface

This book has emerged through a process of enquiry that progressed to surprise and then concern. It was surprising to discover the lack of a concise and dispassionate account of rape law in sixteenth- and seventeenth-century England accessible to the non-legal specialist. But it has been concerning to identify that errors of fact and interpretation entrenched over several decades are now commonplace across the academy. While the lack of an accessible reference source has attracted comment among researchers, far-reaching, inaccurate or reductive assumptions have remained unchallenged. The problem has particularly plagued the world of literature—where rape has sensationalised verse, myth, romance and drama since classical times—but also occurs in the fields of social history, gender studies and sociology.

Once the extent of misinformation became apparent, it was untenable not to pursue it. The process of reviewing and identifying mistaken assumptions alongside law and commentary is relatively straightforward. Less straightforward is how to confront the network of misapprehension that has become established. Factual error, limited reading and misunderstanding of historical sources have led to reiterations and embellishments that have grown exponentially over the decades, ranging from simple restatement of a single incorrect fact to chapter-long analysis based on misreading. The situation is not helped by differing interpretations of the rape statutes among legal professionals from medieval times to the present. It is not possible to alert those exploring the subject of rape in the sixteenth and seventeenth centuries to the danger lurking in ostensibly authoritative critical works without identifying where and what it might be. As far as possible, only indicative examples of common mistakes, and particularly significant, or extensively cited misreading are discussed.

The following chapters are intended to draw attention to the hazards that have contributed to this situation in order to encourage a fresh, more nuanced and less polarised approach to a complex and intractable subject.

London, UK Helen Barker

Acknowledgements

I would like to thank Kate McLuskie for her wisdom, guidance and patience during the research that led to this book. Thanks too to Martin Wiggins and Helen Hackett for encouraging me to publish and to my editor at Palgrave, Emily Russell, for giving me the opportunity to do so. I am very grateful to Palgrave's anonymous reader for invaluable and constructive insights and to Claire Johnson for her diligent reading and comments on the draft. I am very aware of having neglected friends, and I am thankful for their patience and quiet encouragement during this undertaking. Most importantly, the whole process has been made immeasurably easier, in countless ways, thanks to the oversight, observations, endless support and outrageous humour of my husband.

Contents

Abbreviations and Conventions

Quotations from early printed works retain the original spelling, punctuation and capitalisation. I/j, u/v, and long s has been silently amended.

The following abbreviations have been used:

BL	British Library
EEBO	Early English Books Online
ESTC	English Short Title Catalogue
OED	Oxford English Dictionary
STC	Short Title Catalogue

CHAPTER 1

Critical Context and History

Abstract Since the 1980s, across the humanities, non-legal specialists seeking an accessible exposition of rape law in the early modern period have come to rely on a limited range of sources. Two in particular have become ubiquitous: Nazife Bashar's 1983 essay "Rape in England between 1550 and 1700," and the seventeenth-century treatise, *The Lawes Resolutions of Womens Rights*. Yet both contain errors of accuracy and/or interpretation that are now commonplace. Bashar's piece also promotes a direct, anachronistic equation between low prosecution rates and patriarchy. The chapter identifies how and where misreadings of statute law arising from both sources have occurred. It also finds that attitudes to both crime and victims are more representative of the legal and cultural context than Bashar allows, and that prosecution and conviction for murder also produced equivocal results. However, church courts record numerous instances of women, usually of lower social status, accused of a sexual misdemeanour in situations we would now recognise as rape. The records indicate how early modern attitudes deterred women from bringing complaints. Yet the conviction and execution of the Earl of Castlehaven shows that in certain circumstances rape could be dealt with according to the full extent of the law.

Keywords Nazife Bashar • The Lawes Resolutions • Rape law • Church court records • Earl of Castlehaven

H. Barker, *Rape in Early Modern England*,
https://doi.org/10.1007/978-3-030-82609-3_1

The Critical Context

Rape is a crime, and crime is governed by the law extant at any particular time in history. Law in theory and practice is a product of the politics, religion and learning that underpin prevailing cultural beliefs. During the early modern period, common law was evolving from ancient and statute law, while public morality—sexual morality—was the concern of canon law. These all contribute to a context that is fundamental to the definition and meaning of rape in the period. Misunderstanding afflicts the subject across the academy in the fields of gender studies, literature, sociology as well as social history. Much of the ongoing confusion still arises from Bashar's 1983 essay "Rape in England"; some comes from independent misreadings of historical treatises and handbooks, without an appreciation of their status. *The Lawes Resolutions* identifies relevant rape statutes and provides commentary, and so it has proved a beguiling, but potentially misleading source.[1] It is a piece of legal writing from the past that has become embedded in critical writing of the present. However, Chap. 4 demonstrates that the status of the treatise is doubtful: it was a speculative project aimed at exploiting the emerging print industry. Its legal guidance on rape should be treated with caution, while its representation of the legal statutes can be misleading. Those seeking an accessible summary of the law and its context need to be aware not only of what it says but its ambiguities and inconsistencies. That is the aim of Chaps. 2 and 3, respectively; they review the ancient, medieval and common law, and the full sequence of rape statutes, identifying where misunderstandings have arisen in modern criticism. But first, in order to displace unchallenged but erroneous assumptions that have taken hold over some forty years, the remainder of this chapter locates the discussion in a context of interdisciplinary criticism and historiography.

Despite the passage of time, the impact of Bashar's essay should not be underestimated. It is the secondary source most commonly cited by non-legal specialists on the subject of early modern rape law, while *The Lawes Resolutions* is a similarly popular source.[2] Bashar was breaking new ground in 1983 when a dearth of historical information about rape was intrinsic to feminist concerns about the politics of the subject, and methodologies

[1] Bashar, 'Rape in England', 28–42; T.E., *The Lawes Resolutions*: the treatise is the subject of Chap. 4.

[2] Google Scholar shows citations for Bashar as some hundred and forty, and *The Lawes Resolutions*, approximately of a hundred.

were untested. Her analysis of rape has provided a ready source across the academy for those engaging with social history of the period, and the significance of her contribution is borne out by its enduring influence. However, her reading of the legal statutes is faulty and interpretation of historical evidence is presented within a monolithic narrative of gender opposition that is anachronistic and tends to overshadow the wider historical context and limit the potential for enquiry. Yet her assertions have persisted without challenge or corroboration.

Of course, not all misreadings arise from Bashar: either in conjunction with her essay, or separately, critics have sought out the legal statutes and various seventeenth-century legal treatises or handbooks—but often without essential context. Erroneous interpretations have, again, gone unchallenged, become commonplace, and been compounded by further error. As a result, it is not only specific citations of Bashar and/or *The Lawes Resolutions* that pose a trap for researchers but reliance on subsequent critics who have accepted authority of the two works. Literary critics are predominant among those who have sought a legal background against which to write about rape and there is clear frustration at the lack of a comprehensive exposition of early modern rape law. Numerous articles and chapters have been devoted to individual works of literature in which rape occurs—in particular William Shakespeare's *The Rape of Lucrece* and *Titus Andronicus*. But only the onset of the twenty-first century brought two monographs focusing primarily on rape and early modern literature. The first, Jocelyn Catty's *Writing Rape, Writing Women in Early Modern England: Unbridled Speech*, was followed by Barbara J. Baines's *Representing Rape in the English Early Modern Period*. Karen Bamford encompasses rape in her monograph, *Sexual Violence on the Jacobean Stage*.[3] Catty, Bamford and Baines each devote a section to rape and the law, and use Bashar as a significant source. For subsequent writers, these three works assume an updated authority and are regularly cited instead of, or alongside, Bashar. With the realisation that on average these, in their turn, are each cited in excess of a hundred times, the exponential spread of misinformation and the necessity to expose the unstable foundation on which much discussion of early modern rape law is based becomes clearer.[4]

[3] Although many critical citations are of the 1999 edition of Catty's, *Writing Rape, Writing Women*, the relevant reprinted chapters are substantially unchanged. Subsequent references in this book are to the 2011 reprint.

[4] Number of citations based on Google Scholar.

Other substantial studies remained few. Several of the critics who have approached the subject through literature have noted a lack of focused engagement. Catty acknowledges the lack of a "comprehensive study of rape in English literature in the early modern period," contrasting the extent of material on the "accounts of rape in Medieval French literature."[5] Elizabeth Robertson and Christine M. Rose brought out their collection, *Representing Rape in Medieval and Early Modern Literature*, in 2001. Their introduction notes that "[s]urprisingly few books have been devoted to theorising rape," and "[l]ittle theoretical work has been done on representations of rape."[6] In 2003, Linda Woodbridge and Sharon Beehler's collection, *Women, Violence, and English Renaissance Literature* was published. Again, the contents comprise different types of violence and genre so that rape does not predominate. It also contains examples of misleading interpretations of rape law and further authorial misinterpretation that compound existing errors. Lee Ritscher's *The Semiotics of Rape in Renaissance English Literature* (2009) provides an opening chapter on rape law. But from ancient law and the thirteenth-century Statutes of Westminster, her coverage jumps to the late sixteenth century, omitting important stages in between. Nor does she acknowledge the contribution of other writers in the field such as Catty, Baines and Bamford.

Reacting to the critical stasis, in 2009, Amy Greenstadt described the failure of feminist critical practices that were trapped in the opposing positions of "human intentionality" (which she sees as "outmoded") and "a critique of intention" (which invites the very scepticism it seeks to overturn). Her recourse was to displace rape from focal subject to analogy.[7] It seems that the narrative established around early modern rape has left little apparent scope for further analysis. At the same time, those wishing to explore the subject express surprise and frustration at the lack of accessible legal analysis and criticism. Regardless of discipline or ideology, the exposition of the law and the pitfalls surrounding its theory and interpretation set out in the following chapters is intended to allow critics to approach the subject with renewed interest and confidence.

[5] Catty, *Writing Rape, Writing Women*, 2.

[6] Robertson and Rose, eds., *Medieval and Early Modern*, 4. In Robertson and Rose, two essays provide useful footnotes on sources of the law: Cannon, 'Chaucer and Rape', 275 n. 5, 277 n. 13–16, Greenstadt, 'Rapt from Himself', 344–46 n. 25. A later version of Greenstadt's essay can be found in Greenstadt, *Gendering Intention*, 29–55.

[7] Greenstadt, *Rape and the Rise*, 4–5.

Criticism and Methodology

In an early modern society, where the very importance attached to female chastity allowed the ultimate capital penalty for rape, the law was, apparently, rarely invoked. Bashar interprets a lack of prosecutions for rape as evidence of the oppression of women as an adjunct to male "hypocrisy." It is, indeed, incontrovertible that rape in the early modern period (as now) was characterised by low prosecution rates, and that women endured a secondary social status. Bashar notes that "rape usually constituted less than 1 per cent of all indictments." Yet, she argues, there seemed to be no like reluctance to execute thieves or murderers.[8] However, when scrutinised in the context of social order, the priorities of the crown and the structures of family, wealth and power—as well as statistically—the assumption is fallible.

The challenge when discussing rape in early modern England today is how to treat the subject historically while negotiating the gender politics surrounding the topic. From a historical perspective, any commentary on the incidence of rape relies on sufficient cases having been brought to court to be statistically meaningful. It also requires the contextual evidence in which to place such statistical information. That evidence is scant. Low prosecution figures alone can neither be assumed to indicate under-reporting of the crime nor, without supporting evidence, can they necessarily be taken to indicate the conscious manifestation of misogyny perpetuated by all-male institutions. Nor can it be assumed that these factors are not present. Bashar's specific assertions about the law's contributory role in failing to protect women are vulnerable in three respects: methodology, representation of the law and social context.

In terms of methodology, Bashar presents the fact of few recorded prosecutions and convictions for rape, and her analysis of gender politics—that of patriarchal hypocrisy and abuse—as a self-evident dependency. When other historians express caveats about the quantity and quality of documented evidence of the crime from the period, she finds the male academia guilty of "shun[ning] the subject" of rape. J S Cockburn comes in for particular criticism for "dismissing" the crime for yielding too small a sample from which to identify a pattern of offences: "It seems that rape is too risky, too contemporary, too political a subject, to be dealt with

[8] Bashar, "Rape in England," 41, 34, 40.

comfortably by the present-day male historian."[9] This assertion enjoyed credence even with those adopting a more balanced position in the debate such as Roy Porter who used Bashar's quote to introduce his essay "Does Rape have a Historical Meaning?" However, he argues that male authority securely entrenched in traditional societies without "much need for the 'surplus repression' that endemic rape threats would have conferred."[10] E W Ives, among others, warned against over-reliance on prosecution statistics:

> The evident truth [is] that the incidence of prosecutions is no good measure of law enforcement. 'No prosecutions' may mean one hundred per cent deterrent or, equally, inaction; the explanation could also be an offence out of fashion, misleading statistics or changes in enforcement.[11]

Of course, the idea of an "offence out of fashion" underpins Bashar's concern. Criticism of her male colleagues may have been apposite in relation to the politics surrounding feminism and the various historicist criticisms at the time. However, the discomfort she perceives is apt if rooted in the need for statistical validity—in methodology.

Cockburn noted the "comparatively inefficient nature of law enforcement…in the late sixteenth and early seventeenth centuries." He quoted Edward Hext, a Somerset magistrate and clerk in Star Chamber, as suggesting that "in 1596…80 per cent of all criminals evaded trial'. In his analysis of crime Cockburn considered indictments laid at Essex, Hertfordshire and Sussex assizes. He chose these 'because of the survival and accessibility of their records." He warned: "They should not be viewed as a microcosm of the whole of England. Their proximity to London, if nothing else, ensures that the experience of these counties differs to some extent from that of the country at large."[12] Bashar draws on his work and on similar records, presumably for similar reasons of accessibility. When the statistic that rape represents 1% of all indictments at assizes and quarter sessions is placed in conjunction with those of Cockburn's magistrate, the fact that there is little material evidence on which to draw conclusions about rape in the period is not only inevitable but creates considerable space for speculation about the actual incidence of the crime and the

[9] Bashar, 'Rape in England', 28, citing Cockburn, 'The Nature and Incidence', 58.
[10] Porter, 'Historical Meaning?' 216, 223.
[11] Ives, 'Agaynst taking awaye', 30–31.
[12] Cockburn, 'Nature and Incidence', 50–52 (50, 51).

reasons for its invisibility. And, as Cockburn implies, speculation can be dangerous.

But the question of poor evidence is not confined to prosecution statistics. And if rape was under-reported, then so were other crimes, and easy assumptions about the under-reporting of rape must be treated with caution. Cockburn explained that "a majority of criminal court records have been lost or destroyed; and the few that remain are often cryptic and open to various interpretations," but sufficient records survive from 1559 onwards "to allow limited quantification."[13] In addition, he argued that the inaccuracy of the details recorded on those indictments which survive is so rife that possibly half of indictments could have been successfully challenged and dismissed "*ignoramus* (we do not know)" at the assizes. However, his observations reinforce the need for great caution when handling the data.

On the other hand, Bashar takes the low rate of recorded rape prosecutions as indicative of a patriarchal legal system that was prepared to consider prosecution almost exclusively when it threatened property or inheritance arrangements: women represented a potential asset to be disposed of in an advantageous marriage. Rape would render them unchaste and unmarriageable—their personal violation was considered a secondary matter; and women without property were, she suggests, of little consequence.[14] There is general agreement that rape was under-reported, and it is a matter of fact that the emphasis of statute law was on protecting the integrity of family estates against the loss of the material value attached to heiresses. Bashar makes a broad assertion without regard to the history and circumstances through which the law evolved, or the complexities of the law itself. Caroline Dunn points out that the medieval world would not have recognised the personal or emotional impact of rape on a woman—which is not the same as assuming that the male members of the family were likely to be unsympathetic. But, for a man, the loss of a woman's chastity meant "loss of a marriageable daughter, spousal services, and possibly the wife's landed property." Rather than being viewed as possessions, Dunn suggests that women were "measured by the power and status of their male relatives." Bearing in mind the rape statutes originated in the thirteenth century, she points out that it is anachronistic to focus on judicial convictions as the only satisfactory outcome: financial settlements

[13] Cockburn, 'Nature and Incidence', 50; see also Sharpe, *Crime*, 53–54.
[14] Bashar, "Rape in England," 42.

"were viewed differently in the Middle Ages from…today" and that such arrangements persisted into the early modern era.[15] The law evolved—and became increasingly complex—by addition and amendment to those statutes. During an era when any notion of psychological trauma would be an anathema and injury was measured in terms of physical harm or loss, financial settlement, rather than the death of the accused, often suited the parties involved.

Geoffrey Quaife's monograph, *Wanton Wenches and Wayward Wives*, which involved retelling cases involving sexual assault, is also an object of Bashar's ideological criticism. An attack might be justified if made simply on the grounds of its prurience; however, Bashar criticises his failure to "speculate that the historical record may not be a reliable mirror of reality." Specifically, she is disappointed that, in his work on quarter session records, he made no attempt to identify the incidence of older women (as opposed to young girls) featuring as rape victims as both an anomaly and as evidence of under-reporting.[16] While assuming another historian should automatically subscribe to her own theory, she proposes something she has already deemed to be merely a source for *speculation* (the reasons for under-reporting) as *evidence* to support an overarching ideology of male oppression. It is a position that also fails to take account of the straightforward provisions of the law: after all, sex with a child under age was *de facto* rape.[17] Such cases were not open to the subjective, or culturally determined judgements about the moral weakness of women or biological misconceptions surrounding pregnancy, and are therefore more likely to appear in the statistics of successful prosecution.[18] These factors provide a contrary explanation to her assumption that Quaife's work revealed a particular proclivity among Somerset men for sexual assault in general, and against children in particular. Since his work was a specific study of Somerset, it is likely that his findings might be geographically more generally applicable should records be available.

The opposition between Bashar's finding of hypocrisy and the reluctance of her fellow (male) historians to draw similar conclusions brings historiography itself into the debate. As far back as 1977, interdisciplinary tension was apparent, when Edward Shorter began his article, "On Writing

[15] Dunn, *Stolen Women*, 42, 52, 193.
[16] Ibid., 28–29.
[17] On the age of consent and controversy about the violation of children, see Chap. 3.
[18] On rape and conception, see Chap. 2.

the History of Rape" as follows: "I am going to criticize *Against Our Will*, writing from my vantage point as a historian." Susan Brownmiller's book is one which he acknowledged to be "an important substantive contribution to a subject as well known to conventional scholars as the dark side of the moon."[19] Brownmiller's work is particularly pertinent: she is a source for Bashar and is also directly cited by subsequent critics. However, it was not Brownmiller's arguments themselves with which Shorter wished to take issue, but her lack of historical methodology in reading the present back into the past. He challenges her assumptions about "the *nature* of rape in times past," and her failing to note "an apparent *decrease* in the incidence of rape over the past century."[20] His own proposal of rape in past cultures as attributable to "sexual frustration," arising from the apparent assumption "that male sexuality is a constant," Porter pointed out, is also contentious, being guilty of the same anachronistic error.[21] In addition, Shorter's data spanned not only several geographic locations (France, Denmark and Toronto) but the First World War and the influenza pandemic in its aftermath. However, the problem of history concerning Shorter was not the dearth of historical evidence, but methodology and interdisciplinary protocols. It is not simply the charge that Brownmiller was guilty of bad history, but as a non-historian she was attempting to create a history of rape for a specific ideological purpose: to prove that it has always been deployed consciously as a means of social control by men to oppress women.

While Bashar challenges the motivations of colleagues such as Cockburn and Ives, she is obliged to employ the same statistics they consider unviable and geographically unrepresentative. However, her statistics are not always presented within coterminous periods and geographical areas. In one instance, they encompass the five home counties for the period 1558–1700; in others, period or place are selective.[22] This

[19] Shorter, 'On Writing', 471; Brownmiller, *Against Our Will*.

[20] Shorter, 'On Writing' 472.

[21] Porter, 'Historical Meaning?' 219; Shorter, 'On Writing' 474.

[22] While surviving records are limited, those for the home counties are cited by Bashar (as well as Cockburn and others) because of their relative completeness. It is therefore unhelpful that Bashar combines different counties, and different periods of time, to support her arguments. For example, she takes data from Sussex for the period of the reign of Elizabeth I (1558–1603), and Hertfordshire for 1573–1603, 33–34; 1558–1700 in Sussex, "Rape," 34; 'the five home counties between 1558 and 1700', 34–35, 37 (34); and Kent for 1558–99, Ibid., 40. Against this background she elaborates particular points, variously discussing indictments, convictions and penalties.

provokes the question that, since the information is available, why is the data not tabulated in full? The apparent lack of consistency raises the question of whether the narrative of gender opposition has superseded methodological objectivity. The statistics of comparative prosecution, conviction and penalty are revealing. Bashar compares Kent burglary and rape figures for 1558–1599 when burglary statistics show 150 tried, of whom [approximately] 80% were convicted. A total of 122 of those convicted were punished: 88 were hanged, and 34 granted benefit of clergy. For rape in the same period, she quotes 26 tried, 4 hanged, and 2 granted clergy.[23] We have to assume the 6 either hanged or given clergy represent the total number convicted. The statistics are used in support of her assertion of reluctance by the judiciary to hang a man for a sexual crime against a woman. However, although they are extremely limited, they also make a different point. The perceived discrepancy between rape and other crimes is greater between the proportions of those prosecuted who were convicted, than between the proportions, once convicted, who were then hanged. The burglary figures show that the 88 hanged represent 59% of the 150 tried and 73% of the 122 convicted. Assuming a conviction figure of 6 for rape, the statistics for capital punishment are 15% of the 26 tried but 67% of those convicted. Bashar uses data elsewhere in the essay that adds the following information: for the home counties from 1558 to 1700 she quotes 274 cases of rape, giving 45 convictions and 31 hangings.[24] This gives a 16% conviction rate, with those hanged representing 11% of the total tried, and 69% of convictions. They follow a similar pattern as those for Kent alone. Based on these figures, the willingness of the judiciary to hang a man for a sexual offence against a woman takes on a different hue. They show that once convicted, the percentages of capital punishments for rape and burglary are much closer (69% and 73%, respectively). Any disparity in treatment of the crimes would seem to embody the same controversy that endures

[23] Bashar, "Rape in England," 40. On benefit of clergy as a means to escape capital punishment, see Chap. 3.

[24] Ibid., 34.

today: that of gaining a conviction, rather than of applying a harsh penalty once convicted. The causes might lie partly in cultural ideology, but also in the law of evidence.[25]

Although expressing dismay at the apparent reluctance to convict a man for rape in comparison to murder, Bashar does not make a statistical comparison with murder. Yet we should bear in mind that not all murderers were subject to capital punishment either. Similarly to rape, the law was not necessarily straightforward. From the sixteenth century, homicide encompassed murder with malice aforethought, manslaughter, justifiable killing (e.g. self-defence or accidental), and might attract pardons.[26] Alternative punishments to hanging were not uncommon. In her study of murder in the early modern period, K.J. Kesselring gives an example of statistics for Cheshire in the 1620s, showing that, for those convicted for felonies (capital crimes) of all sorts, 166 were hanged, representing 22% of the total accused. In Middlesex, for each of the ten years after 1609, an average of 70.4 were hanged: she finds the figures particularly "striking," since an average of only 10.3 of those were charged with murder or manslaughter in each those years. Interestingly, she finds that the option to convict for manslaughter rather than murder, and options other than a death penalty, led to an increase in conviction rates over those of medieval times. However, she notes that "[m]ost of the condemned suffered for crimes against property, not homicide."[27] Crucially, again, property was a predominant concern. Kesselring continues:

> While those who stole goods of relatively small value might find themselves sentenced to die, those who caused a serious amount of physical harm, and even those who attempted murder, did not. What was being criminalized as felonious behaviour, offensive to king and to the public, was killing, not assault or physical harm.[28]

[25] Without clear caveats, there is a danger of being accused of the same abuse of methodology and statistics as Bashar for several reasons: regardless of the inclusion of as wide a range as possible, historians find too few rape cases from which to identify patterns, and those used here represent an even more limited range of the few; the Kent rape statistics are presumably duplicated in those of the home counties as a whole, and the expanded periods do not coincide. However, as well as indicating an alternative scenario to that of Bashar, the suggestion highlights Bashar's selective and apparently incurious use of data, as well as emphasising its unreliability.

[26] Kesselring, *Making Murder Public*, 19–20.

[27] Ibid., 25.

[28] Ibid., 128, 129.

While drawing a distinction between murder and manslaughter, her observation also underlines the emphasis that common law placed on material goods and their value—a far easier injury to measure than physical harm, and of greater interest to those with goods to lose. As fines and compensation overtook physical punishment, awards would be assessed relative to wealth. Psychological trauma was not recognised and therefore could not be compensated.[29]

Rape Law: Theory and Practice

As a corollary to her interpretation of the statistical evidence, Bashar observes an apparent disparity between what rape law said as opposed to what it did. She points to "the gap between the law's occasional declarations on the heinousness of rape and its treatment of rape in the courts." Her explanation for the low prosecution and/or conviction rates is one of a straightforward legal double standard symptomatic of the patriarchal exploitation of women.[30] Precisely who represents "the law" generally in her assertion is not clear: earlier, she lists legal commentators from the medieval Glanvill, to the nineteenth century's Pollock and Maitland to support her perception that the law failed to meet their expectations of it. She asserts that, because rape was considered a serious crime, these lawyers "assumed that rape…would be actually punished as a matter of course", and cites the sixteenth century jurist Sir Anthony Fitzherbert as deeming rape "to be more important than any property crime" because of its status as "nexte unto murder."[31] When returned to their fuller context, Fitzherbert's words confirm his concern at the offence against the person ("whiche is to ravyshe a woman agaynst her wyll…wher she dyd not assent before"), but it is not exclusive: it includes the possibility of coercion, and extends to elopement—which is a property crime ("though she consente after the acte done, yet is it felony").[32] And as we will see from Chap. 3, there is considerable lack of clarity and flexibility in the interpretation of the statutes of rape, elopement and abduction. It is not the sentiment

[29] Alexandra Shepard, *Accounting for Onesself*, gives an extended account of how witness in church courts described their worth by means of their goods, land, cash and income.

[30] Bashar, "Rape in England," 41, 42.

[31] Ibid., 32–33 (32).

[32] Fitzherbert, *The newe boke*, fol. cxxv. Fitzherbert cites *Statutes* I, (1810), 87, 13 Edward I, the Second Statute of Westminster (Westminster II), c. xxxiv, 1285, in support of his statement.

behind his condemnation of the proven crime that is relevant so much as the definition and determination of the offence.

From a modern standpoint, when a woman's material value and estate are a component of written law, it is easy to identify the social and material status of the victim and the interests of her family as the dominant concern. We should not forget that various handbooks and commentaries—such as Fitzherbert's—acknowledge the heinous nature of the crime. And the penalty for rape was hanging. Sir Matthew Hale has been much maligned for his statement that rape is "an accusation easily to be made and hard to be proved, and harder to be defended by the part accused, tho never so innocent." Yet, where the penalty for a crime is capital, it is a concern that would seem reasonable in any era.[33] It should be borne in mind that he gives specific examples of false allegations that lead to the statement, and begins by identifying rape as "a most detestable crime." So much so that he ends by calling for the court and jury to exercise, "great care and vigilance," to avoid malicious prosecution or false witness because "the heinousness of the offense many times transporting the judge and jury with so much indignation, that they are over-hastily carried to the conviction." Hale expresses a prevailing unease about the risks of hanging a potentially innocent person for any crime. In the case of rape at that time, it could, after all, only be a man accused of the crime, usually committed in private and without witnesses. It was an anxiety that persisted from biblical times and extended beyond both rape and capital punishment to encompass crime and punishment more generally. A century later, William Blackstone's formulation—that "it is better that ten guilty persons escape than that one innocent suffer"—draws on the example of God's mercy towards the residents of Sodom, recounted in Genesis.[34] In this context, Kesselring's observation of increased convictions for manslaughter when there were alternatives to the death penalty is significant.

Against this background, although the law was made and conducted by men, in pursuit of a crime by men against women, it functioned much in the way it was written and understood at the time. Perceived shortcomings, from a twenty-first-century perspective, might be found not in the

[33] Hale, *Historia Placitorum Coronea*, I, 635–36.

[34] Blackstone, *Commentaries*, IV, 352; Genesis, 18. 23–32: God refuses to destroy Sodom if it is found to be inhabited by ten "righteous" men. See also Epps, "Consequences of Error," 1078–81: the maxim, or variations on it were used by Hale in the seventeenth century, but also, for example, in the fifteenth century by John Fortescue, via Blackstone's influence on American law, by Benjamin Franklin.

(mis)application of the law by the early modern judiciary, but by both the religious and secular cultures in which it operated, but not in the far from unreasonable caution exercised in resorting to condemning a man to death.

Fitzherbert and the other commentators, whose texts Bashar cites, had earned their distinction as lawyers and judges before assuming the authority to publish their various treatises. Those who made the pronouncements against the crime are one and the same as those who, at other times, implemented the law. Their condemnation in commentary is consistent with their fear of hanging one who is innocent, but willingness to hang a man once the offence is proven. Pronouncements by medieval and early modern commentators cannot be dismissed as inconsistent simply because they did not see rape in the same places that we do today. Rather than revealing a double standard, they are not so much inconsistent, as consistent with various social and political pressures, and the law that pertained in that historical time. The difficulty seems to be the enduring dichotomy that rape presents: on the one hand, a concept of unequivocal low thuggery attempting chaste innocence, and on the other, the messy reality it more readily presents.

Regardless of any personal or ideological response to the concept of rape, the need for evidence is imperative—and for early modern women, as throughout history, has proved a particular barrier. Despite acknowledgement throughout the judiciary of the deplorable nature of rape, even in a case involving grotesque brutality, it was often difficult to obtain the necessary level of evidence to secure a conviction. A 1598 Star Chamber prosecution serves to show both the challenges of successful prosecution, but also the attitude of the judiciary to the crime of rape. The case involved the gang rape of a landlord's wife and several maids in a tavern by seven men, resulting in the death of one victim and the permanent laming of another. The bailiff and JP to whom the crime was reported dismissed it as "but a trick of yought," and the culprits fled to France. Only the "unrelenting" pursuit of the case by the Attorney General, Sir Edward Coke, eventually brought the men to justice. The case took over a year, and involved the questioning of numerous witnesses. Coke's determination prevailed and prosecution "at the king's suit" resulted in fines of variously £40 and £200—considerable sums at the time.[35]

[35] Knafla, ed. *Kent at Law 1602*, xxv–xxvi, 30–67. £200 would equate to in excess of 4000 days' wages for a craftsman at the time: see, for example, Gregory Clark, "Average Earnings and Retail Prices, UK, 1209–2017," Table 2, https://www.measuringworth.com/datasets/ukearncpi/earnstudyx.pdf. On rape prosecution, either as a capital felony appealed by the victim, or by indictment at the king's suit, punishable by a fine, see Chap. 3.

In her work on rape acquittal in the late sixteenth and early seventeenth centuries, Garthine Walker identifies the challenges faced by women in successfully prosecuting rape—often despite grotesque injuries:

> rape trials were frequently seen to falter as a consequence of the legal definition of rape, the nature of the criminal justice system and the types of evidence available. This is not to deny the crucial role of misogyny, or at least heavy prejudice against women who charged men with rape. Indeed, such attitudes had almost certainly *already* done their work in preventing most rapes from ever reaching the courtroom.[36]

The cases examined by Walker show how prosecutions were confounded by the lack of direct evidence or witnesses, while the extreme youth of many victims meant their testimony was unlikely to be admissible under the age of fourteen.[37] Dating from 1276, an appeal of rape required two witnesses. Hale accepted that, along with witchcraft, 'of all difficulties in evidence', rape…created the 'greatest difficulty'.[38] And in cases of physical rape—as opposed to the elopement or abduction—unlike murder or "felonious property offences" there was no option to reduce the conviction to one of manslaughter or larceny for those accused of rape. Walker describes a number of brutal cases that ended with acquittal, but at which it was made clear to the court and public, via the press, that the perpetrator was not innocent and, in many cases, was convicted of various crimes of assault, or wounding, or "lewdness." Her investigation of the nature of the rapist also finds a number of successful prosecutions for the rape of both under-age, and mature women.[39]

In the concluding section of her essay, Bashar makes her much-quoted but misleading statement: "Rape came to be seen as a crime against the person, not as a crime against property. Statutes of 1555 and 1597 treated abduction separately from rape, and had the indirect effect of establishing rape and abduction as separate offences."[40] The two sentences have proved

36 Walker, "Rape, Acquittal and Culpability," 140.

37 Ibid., 128.

38 *Statutes*, I, 41, 4. Edward I, *Office of the Coroner*; Hale, *Historia Placitorum Coronae*, II, 289–90.

39 Walker, "Rape, Acquittal and Culpability," 124–135 (127); see also Walker, "Everyman or a Monster," esp. 18–23.

40 Bashar, "Rape in England," 41.

particularly beguiling to later critics seeking a comparison between patterns of legislation and social behaviour—to the extent that they are sometimes represented as accepted wisdom, without attribution. They are, in fact, incorrect. There is no relevant statute of 1555, a fact that might be deemed a mere quibble over transcription, however, neither of the two possibly intended statutes—of 1557–8 nor 1575–6—fulfils the designated role either.[41] As can be seen from discussion of the statutes in Chap. 3, controversy surrounds interpretation of the statutes in relation to rape and abduction. However, Bashar neither specifically identifies the legislation, or a corroborative source for her assertion, nor explains how the two statutes bring about the change she describes. Nor is there supporting evidence of the separation of rape and abduction at this point in history, nor a cultural shift in perceptions of rape as a crime against the person as opposed to property.

But her misreading of the statutes leads Bashar to the misperception that, "in the late sixteenth century, the *legal* [my emphasis] view of rape changed." She then attributes the further decline in prosecutions and convictions between 1550 and 1700 to the alleged change, via an increased readiness of lower class women to bring appeals of rape. These dependent factors are then taken to support her identification of the property value vested in women through marriage as the determinant of the seriousness, or otherwise, with which any rape appeal would be treated. All this is circumscribed by the proposal of a direct relationship between rape law and "an intrinsic and powerful part of patriarchy operated for men against women."[42] The link between marriageability and the 'value' of females is incontrovertible, but here too the argument can be oversimplified. It is clear from statute law that material value in the case of rape is predominantly the concern of those with wealth and power, while those at the lower levels of society faced different cultural and social barriers. However, Bashar's proposal sets up a contradictory dependency between the oppression of women through patriarchy and an apparent cultural change, facilitated by the law, leading to greater recognition of women's personal sexual autonomy. That is not to say the relationship between the material worth of women and the importance attached to rape appeals is any less

[41] *Statutes*, IV, part I, 329 (1819), 4 and 5 Philip and Mary, c. viii, 1557–8; ibid., 617, 18 Elizabeth I, c. vii, 1575–6.

[42] Bashar, "Rape in England," 41–42 (41, 42).

significant, but the evidence invites more subtle insight than a simple transhistorical assertion of patriarchy.

"Rape in England": The Legacy

Against this critical background, it cannot be surprising that scholars continue to struggle with the legal context. Unchallenged—and inaccurate—assumptions are embedded in the discourse and perpetuated via an exponential complex of hundreds of cross-referenced citations. In particular, the commonplace acceptance that legal change was effected by statutes of 1555 [*sic*] and 1597, along with various interpretations Bashar has placed on them. But as deeply embedded is a tacit acceptance of the paradigm in which a low prosecution rate for rape is indicative of a difference between the law in theory and practice, and that the whole is a construct of misogyny.

Among the most influential of the literary critics, Catty acknowledges the dangers of reading history from literature, but in situating her work historically, she accepts Brownmiller's assertion of rape's historical role as "an intrinsic part of Western society's subjection of women." But in discussing the "cultural context," she puts the focus on history, on Bashar's misreading of the statutes and the assumed conflict between legal theory and practice.[43] Karen Bamford, in her study of sexual violence on the Jacobean stage, also cites Brownmiller—in this case, the straightforward correlation between rape and patriarchy. She too relies on both Bashar's data and her claims for the disparity between the law in theory and in practice. And although Bamford, not unreasonably, takes Bashar's statistics to support the accepted thesis that rape was under-reported, she is uncritical in following Bashar's conclusions: she accepts the proportionally higher numbers of convictions for the rape of children, as opposed to adult women, as attributable to ideology rather than acknowledging the exigencies of the law and the limitations of the evidence.[44]

Bamford states her "starting point" as "a feminist understanding of sexual assault as a function of culture, rather than of nature." Although primarily interested in representation and how sexual assault is mythologised, rather than its actuality, she acknowledges its place in

[43] Catty, *Writing Rape, Writing Women*, 11, 2, 13, 14.

[44] Bamford, *Sexual Violence*, 5, and 164–65, note 14, note 17, note 18.

"understanding the ways in which hierarchical, gendered societies actually operate."[45] She is obviously aware of potential academic tensions when claiming to avoid "assigning a single, trans-historical meaning to sexual assault." Historians though, might still be uneasy that she has "assumed that modern studies, and in particular feminist theories of sexual violence in the twentieth century, provide a critical vantage point for examining its representation in Jacobean drama." Those theories which might be appropriate to a comprehensive literary reading are precisely those which have been controversial for a histori*cal* reading of 'the ways in which [...] societies [...] operate' in an earlier era.[46] It is an approach that might be perceived as precariously close to the back-projecting so criticised by historians.

Barbara Baines, too, is caught in the tension between ideology and history. In her *Representing Rape in the English Early Modern Period*, she states her purpose as an "interdisciplinary study" with "relevance for succeeding periods, especially our own." The historically overarching approach obliges her to take issue with Walker's statement that "[t]he meaning of rape is historically and culturally specific," since she finds it "difficult to identify what in the ideology of rape is specific to any particular epoch." Similarly to Miranda Chaytor's psychoanalytic readings of rape narratives, Baines is confronted by the historian's insistence that transhistorical meaning, if indeed possible, requires more than correlation with a past event refocused from the present. If the historical context is irrelevant, her perception of "a great disparity between the text of the law and its legal practice," similarly risks being coloured by legal and social anachronism.[47] It is, then, unfortunate that in setting out her arguments she follows Bashar in contending that the 1555 [*sic*] and 1597 statutes "resulted in, or perhaps contributed to, a shift in the way rape was perceived: no longer as a crime against property but as a crime against the person." However, she identifies the faultline in Bashar's assertion, recognising that rape at the end of the sixteenth century was still very much a

[45] Ibid., 6 (citing Porter, 'Historical Meaning', 235).

[46] Bamford, *Sexual Violence*, 4.

[47] Baines, *Representing Rape*, 2; Walker, 'Rereading Rape', 5; Chaytor, 'Husband(ry), 378–407. Baines's apparent oxymoron describing 'the ideology of rape' (1, 2), adds emphasis to her assumption of rape as a transhistorical phenomenon divorced from history and context.

property crime, and that Bashar's hypothesis was not borne out by the case law.[48]

Baines devotes her second chapter to a history of rape law.[49] She makes extensive use of the common law and legal commentaries, but without acknowledging the changes in statute law and parallel progress between statute and the common law over the centuries. By denying the various commentators their historical framework, she judges medieval and early modern commentary from the same viewpoint, and, similarly to Bashar, condemns both for failing to share that of the twenty-first-century feminist. For example, she frames the attitude of the author of the seventeenth-century *Lawes Resolutions* in terms of modern understandings of "feminist inclinations" and "misogynistic assumption." She wonders that he, like the thirteenth-century justice, Henry of Bratton (Bracton), "seems oblivious to the humiliation inherent in [the] ordeal" undergone by a woman reporting a rape, or that "he seems indifferent to the most crucial of issues: what a raped woman's silence about the rape signifies." Such challenges might have been appropriate to institutions over the past half-century or so, but are likely to have made little social or legal sense to early modern men or women.[50]

It is clear that the influence of Bashar's "Rape in England" is still inescapable some four decades later. But by disregarding the need for valid historical sampling, the cultural context and the process of law-making which invariably evolves (often slowly) in the wake of historical circumstances, there is little obvious space to enrich the discourse of rape without a reliable and accurate historical and legal context.

History

Rather than seeking to force unsustainable parallels between specific legislative changes and unviable statistical trends in early modern rape prosecution, it is more profitable to view any developments in conjunction with several factors throughout a prolonged period of significant historical progress. Writing in the specific context of law, both J A Sharpe and Charles M Gray comment on the massive changes taking

[48] Baines, *Representing Rape*, 62, 63.

[49] The chapter substantially reproduces her paper 'Effacing Rape in Early Modern Representation', *ELH*, 65, 69–98 (1998).

[50] Baines, *Representing Rape*, 64–75, (68, 69). On *Bracton,* see Chap. 2.

place. Sharpe reminds us that "crime…must be understood in its social context," emphasising that early modern England "witnessed one of the major transformations in European history: the transition…from feudalism to capitalism."[51] In Gray's introduction to Hale's *History of the Common Law*, he refers to the latter as "a document of the complex intellectual transformation of the seventeenth century." And that transformation occurs throughout all spheres of knowledge: "in science and philosophy, religion and political theory."[52] When the law is considered alongside such a transformation, together with matters of both governance and the genuine beliefs about the nature of men and women, its theory and practice becomes less polarised. Yet, John Baker is confronted by the fact that despite such an "intellectual revolution," "the Law of England seems…hardly to have changed at all." A background of transformation and inconsistency offers a more complex and interesting position from which to explore competing facets of social history that determined how rape was defined and perceived, than one of polarised gender politics.[53]

Miranda Chaytor adopts a psychoanalytic approach to rape in the later seventeenth century; an important facet of her work is the use made of metaphor by women presenting accusations of rape.[54] Walker admires Chaytor's "pioneering" contribution to "restoring the violence of rape…to its history." But she is concerned at the reliance Chaytor places on today's knowledge and perceptions, and is uneasy at its necessary assumption of rape as an "ahistorical," or a "transhistorical" phenomenon.[55] It is a charge that must inevitably afflict the psychoanalytic critic, identifying the danger of privileging nature over culture, and of anachronistic empathy for the past, armed with the enlightenment of the present day. Walker is acutely aware of the tension between cultural ideology and history. Although observing that "the social history of rape in early modern England could be described as a non-history, a history of absence," in a later study, she takes issue with simplistic models of misogyny and transhistorical parallels.[56] Having noted the lack of consensus among historians about the

[51] Sharpe, *Crime*, 21.

[52] Hale, *History*, ed. Gray, xiii.

[53] Baker, *Oxford History*, vol. 6, 3. Baker, 3–53, gives an extended account of the ideas and humanist influence on society and culture and their bearing on the law.

[54] Chaytor, Husband(ry), 378–407.

[55] Walker, 'Rereading Rape', 2, 3.

[56] Walker, 'Rereading Rape , 1; Walker, 'Rape, Acquittal and Culpability, 140, 141.

reasons for low conviction rates, she explores cultural barriers that might have deterred women from pursuing prosecution of sexual violence. In seeking clarification of how this was understood within and without the legal institutions at the time, Walker explores the way discussion of rape was circulated extensively in print at the same time as newspaper crime reporting was a developing feature of communication. It is a historical and historiographical analysis in which she finds acquittals arose for a number of reasons to do with legal definitions, procedure, evidence and social and personal pressures.[57]

Subsequently, Walker has confronted theoretical explanations of men's propensity to rape, questioning overarching categorisations that propose the answer to an intractable question. She notes our inadequacy to define historical perceptions of the concept of the rapist—or indeed the rapist himself—either in his own time, or as a transhistorical phenomenon, or in the present.[58] In each of her interventions, by illuminating the complexity of the subject throughout history, Walker confounds any attempt to distil the phenomenon into a simplistic, reductive model and so enriches the potential for discussion across the humanities. Her ongoing, extended work into attitudinal and legal changes in the treatment of rape will be invaluable to our understanding of the subject.

Recognising Rape in Historical Records

Walker, Laura Gowing and Bernard Capp are among historians who have noted that the challenges facing women from less privileged backgrounds who endured rape were particularly daunting. Evidence of this pattern comes from the lower courts: the quarter sessions, petty sessions and manorial courts, where ostensibly less serious cases were brought, and particularly from the church courts—the bawdy courts—where sexual impropriety and matters of public and private morality were determined.[59] Not only is the subject matter of their proceedings particularly relevant but their records are more plentiful and therefore represent a more valid

[57] Walker, 'Rape, Acquittal and Culpability, 118, 119, 140.

[58] Walker, 'Everyman or a Monster? 5–13.

[59] See Sharpe, *Crime*, 30–40, for a description of the different levels of court and their respective responsibilities. On the functioning of the church courts, see Ingram, *Church Courts*; on their place in cases of slander, sexual insult and reputation, see Gowing, *Domestic Dangers*. On the assizes and quarter sessions, see Herrup, *The Common Peace*; Walker, *Crime*, 17.

sample than those of the assizes. Chastity was the primary determinant of female morality. For the aristocracy, the primary concern was for bloodline and inheritance, but the loss of reputation or the financial implications of bringing up a child fathered by another impacted throughout society. Lower down the social order, rape was more likely to emerge in the church courts, amidst the social preoccupation with moral conduct, where, perversely, it was often the woman's reputation under scrutiny. Victims were most often maidservants: the perpetrators, their masters.[60]

Christopher Hill also warns that "[t]he proceedings of church courts were conducted in Latin, which few English laymen could understand. Men and women…were put on oath and then compelled to testify, if necessary against themselves."[61] It seems that in cases of sexual assault or rape, one major supplementary source is likely to be mediated by the recorder who is certain to have been male. And, in many cases, he was likely to share with the accused a higher (educated) social status than the victim. He would also inevitably be steeped in the cultural suspicion that a woman's failure to defend herself against assault resided in her will rather than her physical strength. It was a society in which women were considered "weak in reason and highly susceptible to [sexual] sin"; and the *querelle des femmes*—the debate about the nature of women—was in full sway. A background of politics, learning and religion collude in a culture that privileges men at the expense of women to obscure a crime otherwise held to be reprehensible under the law.[62]

In the church court records, accounts describing what we might interpret as rape today are often found not among offences committed by men against women, but as accusations against women. They might be brought against absconding servants, or against women charged with fornication, or 'bearing a bastard'—imposing the financial burden of a fatherless child upon the parish. Or they might be of a woman sued for slander by a man for claiming to have been raped or sexually assaulted by him. Although court records show many instances of an accused woman claiming to have

[60] For a full discussion, see Capp, *When Gossips Meet*, esp. Chap. 2; Gowing, Domestic Dangers, passim.

[61] Hill, *Liberty Against the Law*, 194.

[62] Hall, *The Structure of Love*, 3. Hall connects Aristotelian philosophy through St Thomas Aquinas to its influence on Renaissance beliefs about religion and gender. On the *querelle des femmes*, see, for example, Henderson and McManus, *Half Humankind*; and Wiesner, *Women and Gender*, Chap. 1, 17–49, esp. 24–34, on the debate about women, and ideas perpetuated through religious thinking.

been forced into unwanted sex, the cases rarely translated into an appeal of rape or indictment against the man involved.

Religion, moral codes, social status, women's public and domestic roles and concern about public and private order all shape early modern attitudes to women, and therefore to rape. Religious doctrine is fundamental. Biblical teaching cites Eve's temptation and disobedience as evidence of the frailty of the female character to support notions of women's secondary status and man's natural superiority.[63] The Elizabethan *Homily of the state of matrimony* reinforced the New Testament definition of women as "the weaker vessel" who, as wives, are obliged to obey their husbands.[64] It was also accepted wisdom that women were of lesser intelligence, if indeed truly rational beings, and therefore more susceptible to their "baser passions."[65] In addition, women had to contend with the cultural paradox that men expected to meet and overcome physical resistance to their sexual advances. The sentiment is expressed in John Fletcher's *Bonduca*, in which Caratach famously dismisses the Queen's daughters' desire to avenge rape that occurred in the pre-text of the play, telling them: "You should have kept your legs close then."[66] Women were expected to defend themselves against unequal odds, of both strength and obligation, if they were to avoid an assumption of willing participation—as the ancient notion of bloodied and torn clothing implies. And so a woman's word was likely to be thought less reliable than a man's, and even less so if, as seems usual, she was of lower social status.[67]

[63] See Sommerville, *Sex and Subjugation*, 9–14.

[64] *seconde tome of homilies*, fols 253–263^{r} (fol. 255) [STC 2nd edition 13666]. Additionally, *booke of common prayer* (1603), sig. P2^{r}, contains, 'The forme of solemnisation of Matrimonie' which includes paragraphs on the duties of husbands and wives, to be read, 'if there bee no Sermon'. Reference to the wife as the 'Weaker vessel', and her duty to 'submit' and 'to be in subjection' to her husband, follow at sig. P2^{v}. The wording remains virtually unchanged in the modern *Book of Common Prayer*: the reading borrows from various chapters of the *Bible*, see Anthony Fletcher, *Gender, Sex and*, 60. He explains: 'The phrase "the weaker vessel" originated with William Tyndale's translation of the New Testament into English in 1526 and became common usage during the next hundred years or more'. See, for example, I Peter, 3. 7.

[65] Sommerville, *Sex and Subjugation*, 12, 10. See also Fletcher, *Gender, Sex and Subordination*, 60–82; Stone, *Family, Sex and Marriage*, 136–142; Shapin, *Social History of Truth*, 86–91, discusses the perception of women's inferiority in relation to their veracity.

[66] Fletcher, *Bonduca*, ed. Hoy, III. V. 71.

[67] See Capp, *When Gossips Meet*, 5, 143–149.

It is therefore no coincidence that many reports of sexual violence were told by female servants against masters or members of the household. Servants and employers in early modern society were subject to the law when engaging in a contract. In towns and rural communities, annual contracts with three months' notice on either side were usual, although "pregnant or dishonest servants" were often summarily dismissed. Capp explains that absconding servants might be liable to "severe penalties" under the law, yet they faced a gamut of hardship and abuse in the face of which their position left them helpless.[68] Alice Ashmore's master was a London cook who told her: "Thou art my servant and I may do with thee what I please." His attitude seems not to have been unusual.[69]

A case might, then, first have come to the attention of the courts when a female servant ran away from an intolerable situation, or her pregnancy became obvious. The circumstances might be offered in mitigation of the moral offence of which she was accused, and to determine the identity—and financial responsibility—of the alleged father, but were not considered as evidence of rape. Even where force was alleged, rape would be discounted in a case of pregnancy, since conception was generally regarded as evidence of consent. That is not to say a man's moral misdemeanour went unpunished if acknowledged by either the man himself, or by the court. But the punishment falling to a woman was usually greater than to a man, in addition to the loss of her reputation.[70] For innumerable others who put up with the abuse and did not conceive, the events would remain untold. Court reports indicate there was little more sympathy for victims from other women than from the men who abused them.[71]

It is impossible for us now to judge the merit or veracity of individual depositions. Apart from violence, or threats, men used flattery, bribery, seduction or the prospect of marriage to achieve sexual relations.[72] The women themselves undoubtedly had cause to attempt to mitigate their situation by telling of irresistible force, or to implicate particular men as responsible for their state. Some arranged a "hasty marriage" to

[68] Capp, *When Gossips Meet*, 129–30 (129, 129, note 10). See also Wiesner, *Women and Gender*, 109–110, 113–114.

[69] Capp, *When Gossips Meet*, 145.

[70] Gowing, *Common Bodies*, 13.

[71] See Capp, *When Gossips Meet*, 146.

[72] See Capp, *When Gossips Meet*; Ingram, *Church Courts*, 266. See also, Gowing, *Common Bodies*, 99–101, on the subject of the culture of male force.

unsuspecting husbands: one, whose husband of two days became aware of her state, "told him that 'whosoever had got it, he should father it'."[73]

And so if a raped woman escaped pregnancy, or if a pregnancy could be legitimised within marriage, the dilemma of whether or not to make a complaint created the paradox, by which even a violated woman's reputation was ruined through making public her loss of chastity. In addition, the resort to words was contrary to the ideal of female silence and the modesty it implied: verbal incontinence might suggest a more general lack of feminine virtue. The knowledge that women would be reluctant to speak out can only have increased their vulnerability to sexual violation. Their dilemma was compounded by the risk of a counter-claim of slander from an attacker. In one case cited by Gowing, Isabel Burroughs, a servant, was followed to a bedroom by her master, William Gould, who after "there stryving withe her…had to deal with her." In an ensuing court case, her "mother calls her daughter a whore, but had no word for her master: the only articulation she has for her daughter's experience is through the language of sexual insult." Worse, it was Gould who was suing Isabel, her mother, and a friend of her mother's, Katherine Socklyn, who had discussed the situation with others, and brought in a midwife.[74]

Women faced the yet further bind that a chaste and honest woman was not supposed to have either the knowledge or the vocabulary to describe the sexual attempt against which she was obliged to protect herself. As a result, people framed the stories they told at court in terms of plots about sex and marriage which were already well known from popular literature and the stock characters it provided. The danger of over-familiar use of immodest language encouraged the resort to euphemism and analogy. In Devon in 1612, Margaret Commett, a spinster, explained how William Forde, a carpenter, called her to his house to remove a batch of bread her mother was baking in his oven. She returned to clear the cinders. As Commett was about to leave, Forde:

> took her suddenly about the middle…carried her into his hall, and there set her against the wall and forced her against her will and had carnal knowledge of her body, and she saith she cried out and struggled against him as much as she was able.

[73] Capp, *When Gossips Meet*, 147.
[74] See Gowing, *Domestic Dangers*, 61, 75–76.

Commett's deposition claims her reputation through her work: its domestic nature, her conscientiousness and her altruism in helping others. In formal but euphemistic terms, Commett defines what Forde does, but attempts to preserve her modesty by limiting the description of the incident and her language.[75] It is in this context that Walker emphasises the historically and culturally specific meaning of rape. Stories such as that of Commett are shaped to conform to contemporary legal and cultural expectations of female virtue.[76]

Although Commett's deposition mentions that she cried out, the necessity for a raped woman to cry out to demonstrate dissent does not appear in seventeenth-century legal commentaries or compendia. It might be inferred from Hale who suggests that, similarly to Old Testament law, she might fail to summon help if the alleged rape occurred in a place "remote from people, inhabitants or passengers." On the other hand, the raising of a hue and cry after the event, and the speedy complaint to someone of repute were specified in *Bracton* and continued through into early modern compendia such as Dalton.[77] Notably, men less often cited 'consent' in their defence, but were more likely to claim that they were not present at the time and place, or that even if they engaged in horseplay, they had not gone as far as having sexual intercourse with the woman. For men, there was little shame in indulging in illicit sex, only in acknowledging responsibility for any untoward consequences.[78]

Court records find defamation cases heard at the church courts would often arise from an insult, and most often would concern illicit sexual activity. Married women who committed adultery, or single women who indulged in sexual relations, were readily deemed 'whore'. If members of a woman's household transgressed, she risked the insult 'bawd'. A sexual slur was often an attack on a woman's integrity—and would therefore cast doubt on any complaint she might make. Susan Dwyer Amussen cites, for example, a case in 1566, in which a Norfolk man, Thomas Barne, suggested a witness against him was not credible—as a servant, and one who

[75] Gowing, *Common Bodies*, 93; on use of immodest language, ibid., 83, 90; ibid., *Domestic*, 58.

[76] Walker, 'Rereading Rape', 3–5 (5).

[77] Hale, *Historia Placitorum Coronae*, I, 633; Bracton, II, 415; Dalton, *Country Justice* (1618), 248.

[78] Capp, *When Gossips Meet*, 237.

had borne an illegitimate child.[79] Gowing describes how the language and idiom of insult contributed both to a "moral framework" and to the construction of gender that served a male-orientated society. It was one in which women were complicit: they protected their own moral status by denouncing other women to counter insults and accusations against themselves. Thomasine Hayward prompted this response from Joan Searles: "'I ... did never play the whore with John Knight for a wastcoate and holland smocke'." She implies that Thomasine Hayward had done just that.[80] Although women were at a considerable disadvantage if claiming rape or sexual assault, attitudes to sexual morality and to the expectations of the sexual conduct of men and women, by both men and women, contributed to a considerable barrier for the victims.

Despite their inferior status, women in the community were clearly not meek or prevented from robust social interaction. Although the early modern wife was responsible for running the household, as well as moral oversight of the children and servants, women were also active in the economy at all levels of society. Among the aristocracy, a woman might have responsibility for managing an estate in their husband's absence. Lower in the social order, women undertook roles within and without the domestic household: some pursued trades and professions or were active partners in business with their husbands. Church courts, concerned with public morality, dealt with scolding wives, women brawling, slandering and fornicating. In other words, whether through economic necessity or personal negotiation, women were actively engaged throughout society.[81] Nor were they unfamiliar or reticent in using the courts: for instance, Gowing shows that while consistory court litigation in London grew by approximately 2.3 times between 1572 and 1633, cases brought by women increased from 23.2% to 54%. And it was suggested that by the early sixteenth century, the commissary court was "becoming a women's court." The church courts were, of course, dealing with matters of moral

[79] Gowing, *Domestic Dangers*, 60–65, 105–138, esp. 105–106. Amussen, *An Ordered Society*, 100.

[80] Gowing, *Domestic Dangers*, 1, 76–79 (76).

[81] On the roles undertaken by aristocratic women, see Harris, "My Ladies Chamber," esp. 222–23; on women's work, see Clark, *Working Life of Women*; Mendelson and Crawford, *Women*, 94. See Shepard, *Accounting for Oneself*, for detailed data, compiled from church courts records, on women's description of their contribution to the household economy and business. For a full discussion on church courts and their role in the community, see Ingram, *Church Courts*; Gowing, *Domestic Dangers*.

propriety, not prosecuting felonies, but the frequency with which women had recourse to them indicates that they were unafraid actively to use the courts to uphold their reputation or defend the moral standards of the community.

The Castlehaven Scandal

When cultural and institutional priorities intersect, the outcome might be less clear-cut than simple assumptions about male priority and social status suggest. The infamous scandal which reached public notice in 1631 resulted in the trial, conviction, and execution of the 2nd Earl of Castlehaven. Sodomy and rape were the accusations that eventually caused the downfall of the Earl. But in her detailed account, Cynthia Herrup noticed that both the Earl and the prosecution "kept returning to issues of family and betrayal." She found that "the trial became…a constitutional struggle over the meaning of good paternal governance and good legal practice."[82] An environment of family rancour, adultery, unseemly relationships involving servants and potential corruption of the family bloodline established the Earl's disrepute as head of a debauched household.[83]

The story began when Castlehaven's son, Lord Audley, complained to the Privy Council that he feared he was to be disinherited. Castlehaven had bestowed generous gifts of money, property and personal items on an impoverished servant, Henry Skipwith. He apparently delighted in facilitating an adulterous relationship between Skipwith and his son's wife, Lady Audley, who he hoped would produce a son with whom he could displace Lord Audley as his heir. Lady Audley was the Countess's daughter: Castlehaven's daughter-in-law was also his stepdaughter. At the same time, it was "common fame" in the household that Skipwith was "overfamiliar" with the Countess (Audley's step-mother), whom he also accused of promiscuity.[84] Castlehaven was allegedly a voyeur to the various sexual activities of the household that also involved a "'whore' named Blandina." It further emerged that a previously favourite servant, John Anktill, had married, Castlehaven's eldest daughter, Lucy.[85]

[82] Herrup, *House in Gross Disorder*, 2–3 (3), xiii.
[83] Ibid., e.g., 3, 17, 19–22, 47, 75.
[84] Ibid., 38, 40 (38).
[85] Ibid., 40–41 (41).

Following the investigations into Lord Audley's complaints, a commission, appointed by the King, indicted Castlehaven for sodomy and rape—the rape charge resulting from the Countess's resistance to the Earl's attempts to encourage sexual relations with his favourites.[86] Although the Earl's conviction defines the court's acceptance of the Countess's role as victim, her failure to register any complaint indicates the vulnerability of any woman's position. In accordance with assumptions about women's reliability, neither the Countess nor Lady Audley appeared at the trial, and no female servants were questioned. It was an ideology exploited by the Earl in his defence which relied on assumptions about women's lack of reason, and excesses of sexual desire and deviousness. Interestingly, the judge admonished the defence, saying "that a victim's reputation was irrelevant to the crime of rape." Even so, the social reputations of the two women were tarnished—whether deservedly so or not. Their mother/grandmother, The Dowager Countess of Derby, insisted they repent, sue for pardons and acquire financial support before she would accommodate them. The King brokered the agreement in 1631.[87]

The Castlehaven case provides a rare example of rape law in practice achieving a conviction—and the capital penalty—for the sexual violation of a woman. Possibly, in the eyes of his peers, the Earl's greatest crime was his attempt to corrupt a noble bloodline. However, Herrup's evidence indicates how crucial was the perceived threat to general social order by Castlehaven's failure as an example: as a head of household, as a man and as a member of the aristocracy whose position implied honour.[88] Without the contravention of these predominantly male concerns the matter of rape is more likely to have escaped prosecution.

When the state embraces an overarching system of government, there is a danger that criticism of it becomes meaningless if it is merely a restatement of those characteristics by which the system is defined. Patriarchy necessarily prioritises male interests, so it is unsurprising that matters of specifically gendered behaviour—such as rape—appear unbalanced from the perspective of another historical time. But that does not preclude a more subtle response than the simple abuse of power by one sex deliberately to disadvantage the other. Nor does it require any contradiction

[86] Ibid., 49 p. 18, 43–44.

[87] Ibid., 147–48 (148), 100–101.

[88] Ibid., 20–21, 77–81. See also Fletcher, *Gender, Sex and Subordination*, chapter 7, 126–153 on the code of honour assumed by the gentry.

between theory and practice in order for the law to favour the wealthy and the powerful. The law either works, or is amended, according to the perceptions of those very groups, and according to its effectiveness to deliver their intentions. Any suggestion of a mismatch between rape by men of women in the sense that we might think of it now, and its apparently low priority betrayed by its treatment in early modern law, assumes it had the same meaning in medieval and early modern times as today. It is anachronistic legally, intellectually and socially to respond with twenty-first-century dismay to practices consistent with understandings and priorities from a different era. Church court records amply demonstrate social attitudes to morality, undifferentiated by gender, and in circumstances unallied to wealth and power, that more readily denigrate a woman who has been sexually violated than recognise the crime of rape.

Nor can we be complacent from the point of view of the present, when noting that recognition of the personal impact of rape on the victim appears at odds with its apparent condemnation in legal writings. Changes introduced in the conduct of criminal trials in the late eighteenth century, which might be termed progress, conversely added another barrier for victims of rape. Increasing emphasis was given to the notion of innocence until proven guilty, and that guilt should be beyond reasonable doubt. In the early 1700s, the presence of defence barristers in felony trials was rare, but in the early 1780s, there was a substantial increase. The introduction of counsel transformed the criminal trial to adversarial performances characterised by "aggressive advocacy" and cross-examinations which began the culture of victim-blaming that still prevails today.[89]

Bibliography

Amussen, Susan Dwyer. *An Ordered Society: Gender And Class In Early Modern England*. New York: Columbia University Press, 1993.

Baines, Barbara J. "Effacing Rape in Early Modern Representation", *ELH*, 65 (1998): 69–98.

———. *Representing Rape in the English early Modern Period*. Lampeter: Mellen, 2003.

Baker, John. *The Oxford History of the Laws of England*, vol. 6, edited by John Baker. Oxford: Oxford University Press, 2003- (2003).

Bamford, Karen. *Sexual Violence on the Jacobean Stage*. Basingstoke: Macmillan, 2000.

[89] Beattie, "Scales of Justice," 248, 227–28, 236, 239.

Bashar, Nazife. "Rape in England between 1550 and 1700", in *The Sexual Dynamics of History: Men's Power, Women's Resistance*. The London Feminist History Group. London: Pluto, 1983.

Beattie, J.M. "Scales of Justice: Defense Counsel and the English Criminal Trial in the Eighteenth and Nineteenth Centuries". *History Review*, 9 (1991): 221–267.

Blackstone, William. 4 vols. *Commentaries on the Laws of England*. Oxford: Clarendon Press, 1769.

The Booke of common prayer, and administration of the sacraments and other rites and ceremonies of the Church of England. London: Barker, 1603.

The Book of Common Prayer and Administration of the Sacraments and Other Rites and Ceremonies of the Church of England. Oxford: Oxford University Press [1969 (?)].

Brownmiller, Susan. *Against Our Will: Men, Women, and Rape*. New York: Simon & Schuster, 1975.

Cannon, Christopher. "Chaucer and Rape: Uncertainty's Certainties", in *Representing Rape in Medieval and Early Modern Literature*, edited by Elizabeth Robertson and Christine M. Rose. Basingstoke: Palgrave, 2001.

Capp, Bernard. *When Gossips Meet: Women, Family, and Neighbourhood in Early Modern England*. Oxford: Oxford University Press, 2003.

Catty, Jocelyn. *Writing Rape, Writing Women in Early Modern England: Unbridled Speech*. 1999. Revised reprint, Basingstoke: Macmillan, 2011.

Chaytor, Miranda. "Husband(ry): Narratives of Rape in the Seventeenth Century", *Gender and History*, 7 (1995): 378–407.

Clark, Alice. *Working Life of Women in the Seventeenth Century*, 3rd edition, with a new introduction by Amy Louise Erickson. London: Routledge and Keegan Paul, 1992.

Cockburn, J. S. "The Nature and Incidence of Crime in England 1559–1625: A Preliminary Survey", in *Crime in England 1550–1800*, edited by J. S. Cockburn. London: Methuen, 1977.

Croft, Lyndsay Marie. "'Some Women Love to Struggle': A Cultural and Critical Analysis of Dramatic Representations of Rape in the Late Elizabethan and Jacobean Periods". PhD thesis, Loughborough University, 2007.

Caroline Dunn. *Stolen Women in Medieval England: Rape, Abduction and Adultery*. Cambridge: Cambridge University Press, 2013.

E[dgar] T[homas]. *The Lawes Resolutions of Womens Rights: Or, The Lawes Provision for Woemen*. London: More, 1632.

Epps, Daniel. "The Consequences of Error in Criminal Justice". *Harvard Law Review*, 128 (2015): 1065–1151.

Fitzherbert, Anthony. *The newe boke of justices of peas*. London: Redman, 1541.

Fletcher, Anthony, *Gender, Sex and Subordination in England 1500–1800*. London: Yale University Press, 1995.

Fletcher, John *Bonduca*. edited by Cyrus Hoy, in *The Dramatic Works in the Beaumont and Fletcher Canon*, edited by Fredson Bowers, 10 vols. Cambridge: Cambridge University Press, 1966–1996, IV. 1979.

Gowing, Laura. *Common Bodies: Women, Touch and Power in Seventeenth Century England*. New Haven: Yale University Press, 2003.
———. *Domestic Dangers: Women Words and Sex in Early Modern London*. 1996. Reprint, Oxford: Clarendon Press, 2005.
Greenstadt, Amy. *Rape and the Rise of the Author: Gendering Intention in Early Modern England*. Farnham: Ashgate, 2009.
———. "Rapt from Himself: Rape and the Poetics of Corporeality in Sidney's *Old Arcadia*", in *Representing Rape in Medieval and Early Modern Literature*, edited by Elizabeth Robertson, and Christine M. Rose. Basingstoke: Palgrave, 2001.
Hale, Matthew. *Historia Placitorum Coronae*, 2 vols. 1736. Reprint, London: Professional Books, 1971.
———. *The History of the Common Law in England*, edited by Charles M. Gray. 1713. Reprint, 1739. Reprint, London: University of Chicago Press, 1971.
Hall, Michael. *The Structure of Love: Representational Patterns and Shakespeare's Love Tragedies*. Charlottesville: University Press of Virginia, 1989.
Harris, Barbara J. "The View from My Lady's Chamber: New Perspectives on the Early Tudor Monarchy", *Huntington Library Quarterly*, 60 (1997): 215–47.
Henderson, Katherine Usher, and Barbara F. McManus. *Half Humankind: Contexts and Texts of the Controversy About Women, 1540–1640*. Urbana: University of Illinois Press, 1985.
Herrup, Cynthia. *The Common Peace: Participation and the Criminal Law in Seventeenth-Century England*. Cambridge: Cambridge University Press, 1987.
———. *A House in Gross Disorder: Sex, Law, and the Second Earl of Castlehaven*. New York: Oxford University Press, 1999.
Hill, Christopher. *Liberty Against the Law: Some Seventeenth-Century Controversies*. London: Penguin, 1996.
Ingram, Martin. *Church Courts, Sex and Marriage in England 1570–1640*. 1987. Reprint, Cambridge: Cambridge University Press, 1994.
Ives, E. W. "'Agaynst taking awaye of Women': The Inception and Operation of the Abduction Act of 1487", in *Wealth and Power in Tudor England: Essays Presented to S.T. Bindoff*, edited by E. W. Ives, R.J. Knecht and J.J. Scarisbrick. London: Athlone Press, 1978.
Knafla, Louis A., ed. *Kent at Law 1602*, 3 Star Chamber. Kew: List and Index Society, 2009.
Mendelson, Sara, and Patricia Crawford. *Women in Early Modern England 1550–1720*. Reprint, Oxford: Clarendon Press 2003.
Mills, Janis Jane Darvill. "Early Modern Legal Poetics and Morality 1560–1625". PhD thesis, University of Sussex, 2011.
Porter, Roy. "Does Rape have a Historical Meaning?", in *Rape*, edited by Sylvana Tomaselli and Roy Porter. Oxford: Blackwell, 1986.

Quaife, G. R. *Wanton Wenches and Wayward Wives: Peasants and Illicit Sex in Early Seventeenth Century England*. London: Croom Helm, 1979.

Ritscher, Lee A. *The Semiotics of Rape in Renaissance English Literature*. New York: Lang, 2009.

Robertson, Elizabeth, and Christine M. Rose, eds. *Representing Rape in Medieval and Early Modern Literature*. Basingstoke: Palgrave, 2001.

The seconde tome of homilies. London: Richard Jugge, 1563. STC 2nd edition 13666.

Shapin, Steven. *A Social History of Truth: Civility and Science in Seventeenth Century England*. London: University of Chicago Press, 1994.

Sharpe, J. A., *Crime in Early Modern England 1550–1750*, 2nd edition. London: Longman, 1999.

Shepard, Alexandra. *Accounting for Oneself: Worth, Status, and the Social Order in Early Modern England*. Oxford: Oxford University Press, 2015.

Shorter, Edward. "On Writing the History of Rape", *Signs*, 3 (1977): 471–82.

Sommerville, Margaret R., *Sex and Subjection: Attitudes to Women in Early-Modern Society*. London: Arnold, 1995.

Statutes of the Realm, 12 vols. London: England Record Commission, 1810–1828.

Stone, Lawrence. *The Family, Sex and Marriage in England 1500–1800*, abridged edition, 1979. Reprint, London: Penguin, 1990.

Walker, Garthine. *Crime, Gender and Social Order in Early Modern England*. Cambridge: Cambridge University Press, 2003.

———. "Everyman or a Monster? The Rapist in Early Modern England, c.1600–1750", *History Workshop Journal* 76 (2013): 5–31.

———. "Rape, Acquittal And Culpability in Popular Crime Reports in England, c. 1670–c. 1750", *Past & Present* 220 (2013): 115–142.

———. "Rereading Rape and Sexual Violence in Early Modern England", *Gender and History*, 10 (1998): 1–25.

Wiesner, Merry E. *Women and Gender in Early Modern Europe*, 3rd edition. Cambridge: Cambridge University Press, 2008.

Woodbridge, Linda and Sharon Beehler, eds. *Women, Violence, and English Renaissance Literature: Essays Honoring Paul Jorgensen*. Tempe: Arizona Center for Medieval and Renaissance Studies, 2003.

CHAPTER 2

The Legal Framework

Abstract The evolution of early modern law encompassed a range of geographical and historical influences, from the Bible to Elizabethan politics. Common law precedents, established by custom and usage from ancient and medieval times, coalesced with later statute law. Legal treatises began to emerge following the establishment of written law from the end of the twelfth century. With the advent of print, guidance was abridged and circulated in innumerable handbooks. Varying interpretations, emphases and intentions of the texts allow significant scope for misrepresentation in modern criticism. Sources of confusion include understanding the purpose of a hue and cry, the intractable debate over the definition and use of the terms 'rape' and 'ravishment', the device of marriage to the rapist and early modern beliefs surrounding rape and conception. This chapter identifies how and where errors in criticism have arisen from common law through misreadings of the treatises and handbooks and/or mistaking their legal status. The chapter explains how matters of rape and conception were complicated by Galenic theory, while marriage was surrounded by legal and ecclesiastical complexity.

Keywords Rape and ravishment • Marriage to the rapist • Hue and cry • Rape and conception

H. Barker, *Rape in Early Modern England*,
https://doi.org/10.1007/978-3-030-82609-3_2

Common Law: Ancient, Medieval, Early Modern

Rape law extant in early modern England had its origins in ancient law. It eventually stabilised during Elizabeth I's reign, but interventions throughout its three-hundred-year evolution contribute to a lack of clarity, as do common law practices surviving from ancient times.[1] Looking further back in history, a cultural background to rape law can be found in the Bible. According to the Old Testament, if a woman was betrothed, her rape was punishable by death. But if she was an unattached virgin, a fine was paid to her father, and the rapist and victim were required to marry. A woman was expected to cry out if attacked in a populated area, or else she was deemed complicit and condemned along with the man. And the penalty for consensual loss of virginity before marriage, or for adultery, was the same as that for a rape: death by stoning.[2] Although by medieval times the woman was not condemned if found in any way culpable, elements of Biblical law remain visible in ancient, medieval and early modern common law guidance.

Despite any residual Biblical influence, the mid-seventeenth-century lawyer, Sir Matthew Hale explains the significance of identifying the beginnings of law, and how it is determined. He tells us that Time within Memory begins with the reign of Richard I on 6 July 1189, after which statute law or Acts of Parliament fall within the written law (*Lex Scripta*). Laws made prior to this date are deemed *Lex non Scripta* (unwritten law) and no longer pleadable as Acts of Parliament "because what is *before* Time of Memory is supposed without a Beginning, or at least such a Beginning as the Law takes Notice of." However, those laws that were "now accounted Part of the *Lex non Scripta* being…incorporated thereinto, and become a part of the Common Law…obtain their Strength by meer immemorial Usage or Custom." It seems that the common law (arising from judicial decision, custom or precedent) provided the means by which residual practices carried on to complement written statute law—adding to the complexity—and therefore scope for confusion—with which the modern critic is required to engage.[3]

[1] The law remained substantially unchanged throughout the seventeenth and eighteenth centuries until the death penalty for the crime was repealed in 1840. Toner, *Facts of Rape*, 98.

[2] Deut. 22: 13–30 (AV) sets out the laws in relation to sex outside marriage, adultery and rape.

[3] Hale, *History* ed. Gray, 3–4 (4). For an explanation of the common law, see also, Law, ed. *A Dictionary of Law*, s.v. "Common law."

Henry of Bratton or Bracton, a thirteenth-century justice, authored the eponymous treatise around the mid-1220s to early 1230s. *Bracton* is one among several early legal texts that give an account of the ancient law.[4] The anonymous *Fleta*, dated between 1290 and 1300, appears to be based on *Bracton*, but incorporates law passed under Edward I, and was regarded as an authoritative source of reference by Sir Edward Coke, the late sixteenth- and early seventeenth-century chief justice.[5] Lawyers in later centuries also referred back variously to the treatises *Glanvill*,[6] *Britton*,[7] *Liber Horn* and *The Mirror of Justices*[8] for opinion and commentary on the common law. The ancient law of rape is described in the "Addition" to *Bracton*. The author looks back in history to describe the ancient law of Athelstan. At that time, offences ranged variously from indecorous touching to lying with the victim. The punishments were then graduated proportionately from compensation via the county court, to "loss of…life and members."[9] This ancient law provides context for historical attitudes found in *The Lawes Resolutions* and, via both treatises, in modern criticism.[10]

Coming on to his own historical time, *Bracton* explains the equation by which divine authority is vested in the king and delegated down through his representatives: "all men ought to be subject to the king as surpassing all in virtue and to his ministers as sent from him. Thus divine law agrees to some extent with human."[11] Although public order serves society in general, the law functions as an instrument to serve the crown's interests above those of its subjects. The raising of funds and the imposition of

[4] Bracton, *De Legibus* (*Bracton*), ed. Woodbine, trans. Thorne.

[5] Richardson and Sayles, eds. and trans. *Fleta*, vol. 72; *Oxford Dictionary of National Biography*, s.v. "Fleta (fl. 1290–1300)" (by David J. Seipp), paragraphs 1 and 5. https://doi.org/10.1093/ref:odnb/9716. Accessed 6 April 2021.

[6] Glanville *Treatise on the Laws*, ed. Hall.

[7] *Britton*, ed. Nichols.

[8] Horne, *Mirrour of Justices*.

[9] *Bracton*, II, 418. Going even further back in time, Bracton (ibid.), explains that "By the law of the Romans, the Franks and the English," as well as the punishment of the rapist, his horse, dog and hawk that he owned should also be brutally mutilated and shamed; and by the king's warrant, any fine of "land and money…shall be given to the woman."

[10] T.E., *The Lawes Resolutions*, 378–79.

[11] *Bracton*, II, 359. Earlier in this passage, Bracton describes rape as one of "the lighter crimes": one "who were he present and convicted would lose no more than his members; he sometimes loses his life, on account of his flight." This is not necessarily to suggest a less than serious view of rape, but that it carries a lesser punishment than death unless, as in his example, the offender absconds.

public order both preoccupied the crown in the Middle Ages, just as they continued to do so into early modern times. Both preoccupations influenced the introduction and drafting of various laws—including (as will be seen from the discussion of the statutes in Chap. 3) that of rape.

Ancient custom and practice which persisted alongside the written law particularly concerned the established process to be followed in an appeal of felony. In his exposition on rape, Bracton first sets out the punishment, and how abettors are treated, followed by the process by which a woman should bring her appeal, the wording of it, possible defences to it, and the woman's influence on the punishment. He tells us: "Among other appeals there is an appeal called the rape of virgins." The specific reference to virginity in the naming of the crime is particular to its punishment which is:

> Loss of members, that there be member for member, for when a virgin is defiled she loses her member.... Let him thus lose his eyes which gave him sight of the maiden's beauty for which he coveted her. And let him lose as well the testicles which excited his hot lust. Punishment of this kind does not follow in the case of every woman, though she is forcibly ravished, but some other severe punishment does follow, according as she is married or a widow living a respectable life, a nun or a matron, a recognized concubine or a prostitute plying her trade without discrimination of person, all of whom the king must protect for the preservation of his peace, though like punishment will not be imposed for each.[12]

The passage raises a number of points which are revealing of its contemporary culture: the question of virginity and the equation of a woman's sexual status with the assumed severity of the crime, the assumption that rape is a crime of lust and desire—and that lust is apparently a natural response to female beauty, and the recognition of the law's responsibility to prostitutes. It also confirms the paternalistic relationship between the king and his subjects in which the purpose of the law provides a critical tool for "the preservation of his peace."[13]

In order to resort to the law, a victim must, in turn, follow a clearly defined process in order to bring an appeal of rape:

[12] *Bracton*, II, 414–15.

[13] Post, "Ravishment of Women", ed. Baker, 153, points out that prior to the statutes of Westminster, despite *Bracton*, in practice courts did not support appeals brought other than by virgins.

> She must go at once and while the deed is newly done, with the hue and cry, to the neighbouring townships and there show the injury done her to men of good repute, the blood and her clothing stained with blood, and her torn garments. And in the same way she ought to go to the reeve of the hundred, the king's serjeant, the coroners and the sheriff. And let her make her appeal at the first county court.... Let her appeal be enrolled in the coroners' rolls, every word of the appeal, exactly as she makes it, and the year and the day on which she makes it. A day will be given [her] at the coming of the justices, on which let her again put forward her appeal before them, in the same words as she made it in the county court, from which she is not permitted to depart lest the appeal fall because of the variance, *as is true in other appeals* [my emphasis].[14]

It should be emphasised that the actions required of the woman in response to a rape follow those generally prescribed for any appeal of felony, "for he who wishes to appeal ought to sue properly."[15] With no appointed body to enforce the law, hue and cry was a levy placed on "all [men] who are fifteen years of age and more" in the event of a reported felony. A felon was to be pursued "from estate to estate and from vill to vill," and if he was not apprehended "the entire township [would] be amerced."[16]

The hue and cry and reporting to officials, signs of injury, the precise recording of the words and the details of time and place are common to all felonies. Speedy reporting and consistency in the recording of evidence are adduced to support the legitimacy of the appeal. In cases of wounding, clearly the officials would expect to see wounds. But there is an assumption in cases of rape that the crime equates with the use of force or violence. This, in turn, has implications for determining the question of consent, and the establishment over ensuing centuries of the dangerous corollary (for women) that lack of evidence of violence equates with lack of resistance and, therefore, with consent.[17] However, the historical time is particularly important. Elise Bennett Histed points out: "In an era in history when the population concentrated upon proofs of innocence or

[14] *Bracton*, II, 415.

[15] Ibid., 394. See also Glanville, *Treatise on the Laws*, XIV, chapters 1–8, 171–177, which specifies considerations specific to different crimes.

[16] *Bracton*, II, 327–28 (327), 350.

[17] The question of consent, or its absence, is implied or specified when defining rape law from ancient times. See *Bracton*, II, 416.

guilt such as the ordeals this is quite understandable."[18] The evidence that officials might expect to see depends on the crime, and *Bracton* indicates the sort of detail that should be recorded.

> If it is an appeal of...wounding, what kinds of wounds they were, fresh or old, and in what part of the body and of what length and depth. If the appeal is one of robbery, of what goods, and whether his own or another's. If of coined money he must state the number and kind of coins; if of bullion, its value...if of clothes, their colour and value...if of an animal, then the kind, the coat and the value...If it is an appeal of arson, when it occurred and all the circumstances. If an appeal of rape, then whether garments were torn and whether blood was shed by the ravishment.[19]

In theatrical representation, rape was often indicated in the aftermath by the victim's physical dishevelment in variations of the stage direction: "Enter: *hair about her ears.*" Her physical disarray fulfils the dual purpose of indicating that she has been raped, and her status as innocent victim.[20]

The formula for reporting, and examples of evidence given, support a process designed to meet the expectations the court might have of both behaviour and evidence on the part of both appellant and appellee. In the case of rape, the questions take account of exceptions to the appeal that might be brought by the appellee. These include what might be called a technical exception that applied to other crimes: "that suit was not adequately made." There are five other exceptions specified (in addition, says *Bracton*, to "Many other matters...though I do not now call them to mind"):

> [1] that he did not deprive her of her maidenhood...In that case let the truth be ascertained by an examination of her body, made by four law-abiding women sworn to tell the truth as to whether she is a virgin or defiled. If they say that she is a virgin, the appellee will depart quit of that appeal and the

[18] Histed, "Mediaeval Rape": 758–59. See 759, note 51: "The ordeals, physical trials endured by the defendant in an appeal to God to prove guilt or innocence (by, for example, non-corruption after three days of a hand that has been dipped in boiling water) are not the only indicators of the very physicality of the medieval focus."

[19] *Bracton*, II, 394–95.

[20] See, for example, stage directions: Peele, *David and Fair Bethsabe* ed. Greg, Scene 4, line 351.0; Massinger, *The Unnatural Combat*, in *The Plays and Poems*, ed. Edwards and Gibson, II, 5.2.185.1; Davenport [?], *Dick of Devonshire*, ed. McManaway and McManaway, 2.2.687; Wilson, *The Swisser*, ed. Itzoe, I4.1.0; Davenant, *the Unfortunate Lovers*, 5.1.19, 5.1.30.

> woman will be placed in custody [deemed to have made a false allegation]; if they find that she has been defiled, inquiry must be made as to the guilty party, whether by the appellee or another...[2] He may also except against her and say that he has had her as his concubine and *amica* before the day and year mentioned in the appeal... [3] [or] that he had her and defiled her with her consent and not against her will, and that if she now appeals him it is hatred of another woman whom he has as his concubine, or whom he has married, and at the instigation of one of her kinsmen. [4] He may also except that on the year and day the deed was supposed to be done he was elsewhere....also [5]...on the ground of an omission in the appeal, because she says no more than he lay with her, no mention made of her maidenhood.[21]

There is no separate plea listed in respect of women not claiming rape without loss of virginity. But the severe penalties for rape of virgins, and specific processes required to meet standards of evidence, suggest that within the limits of contemporary social politics, the law seeks to achieve a balance for both the woman and the accused. In doing so, the guidance on exceptions acknowledges the vagaries of human behaviour, but also makes clear that the woman who brings a rape appeal is vulnerable to imputation of her reputation. It introduces the enduring anomaly between the possibility of a woman making a false claim of rape, and the burden of proof being so onerous that the risk to her reputation makes the law itself a deterrent to an appeal.

Common law provided a conduit by which medieval attitudes and practices persisted into early modern England, alongside the shifting priorities of crown and state, to influence the implementation of rape law. Despite its status as unwritten law, the influence of the rules set out in *Bracton* is clear in the early modern legal compendia of the early seventeenth century. Early modern guides like Michael Dalton's *Country Justice* offered lawyers and officials a succinct version of both the relevant common law and statute law. For instance, in all editions of *The Country Justice* published between 1618 and 1630, and still extant in the eighteenth-century editions, remnants of the earlier rules are recognisable. In particular the necessity to raise a hue and cry remains—without specifying that the victim should show bloodied and torn clothing—along with the guidance

[21] *Bracton*, II, 417, 416–17.

that a man might successfully plead that a woman was previously his concubine, and that a prostitute is protected by the law.[22]

Some Sources of Confusion

Contrary to their purpose, however, inconsistent terminology throughout both the treatises and statutes, together with the residual medieval common law practices, has contributed to modern misunderstandings. Four such topics are worth exploring before progressing to discussion of the statutes in the next chapter. First, the misinterpretation of the requirement for a hue and cry. The second is the semantic muddle which surrounds the use of the terms 'rape' and 'ravishment'. Third is the ancient practice of giving a rape victim the option to marry her rapist. The fourth topic is the assimilation into law of the belief that rape was incompatible with conception.

Hue and Cry

When discussing William Shakespeare's play *Titus Andronicus* in the context of the actions required by common law when a woman reports a rape, Kim Solga bases a fundamental strand of her argument on the "theatricality" of the woman's actions. Under the heading, of "Hue and Cry," she argues that a slight difference in the wording between early treatises of Bracton and Glanvill, and *The Lawes Resolutions* indicates a "shift: it encourages women to body forth the implicit theatricality of – the performance of innocence implied by – the scripts in the earlier treatises."[23] However, there are two problems with this argument. The first is factual. Unfortunately it conflates the medieval emphasis on physical display of

[22] Dalton, *The country justice* (1618), 247–48; (1619), 256–57; (1622), 256–57; (1626), 281–282; (1630), 281–82; (1705), 392–93. The 1618 edition, 256, for example, also specifies the responsibility on "every man" to join the hue and cry, or otherwise "appeare before the Justices of gaole delivery." Some fifteen editions or imprints were printed from 1618 to the end of the century, and it continued to be published into the eighteenth century. The work in its various editions is referred to as *The Country Justice* hereafter. Of various other handbooks commending themselves to justices of the peace, all quote very similar definitions of the law, and most are based on the work of a collaborative group of lawyers. For instance, *A manuall or analecta* [or] *The compleat justice* was published in several editions until 1681, variously indicating its main source or authorship as lawyers Richard Crompton, William Lambarde and Dalton, along with one Richard Chamberlain, or are unattributed.

[23] Solga, *Violence Against Women*, 38.

evidence with the hue and cry—the pursuit of the felon. Both components were essential to the successful prosecution of *all* cases of felony, not just rape.[24] However, Solga appears to mistake the hue and cry as a required rehearsal and display of evidence by a raped woman. Obviously, the victim had to demonstrate good cause to raise a hue and cry. But although both Glanvill and Bracton require the rape victim to accompany the pursuit, it otherwise comprised men. The abduction of the heroine, Florimell, in John Fletcher and William Rowley's 1623 play, *The Maid in the Mill*, indicates the public would be aware of the requirement. Florimell's brother, Bustofa, calls for a "Hue and cry" to be raised, while Julio (a noble) promises to "fill the Countrey" in her pursuit.[25] The second problem rests with assumptions about authority of *The Lawes Resolutions*. Chapter 4 explains its very limited circulation and negligible influence in its own time. Dalton's popular *Country Justice*, on the other hand, states simply: "A woman that is ravished, ought presently to levie huy and cry, or to complaine thereof presently to some credible persons as it seemeth." It does not choreograph a performance. If Solga's argument is applied to Dalton, by early modern times the law required less of a spectacle than in medieval times, not more.[26]

Rape or Ravishment

It is already apparent from *Bracton* that the words 'rape' and 'ravishment' are both used in the same context. Attempts to distinguish between the meaning, in law and commentary, of rape and ravishment, between the various conjugations of *raptus* and *rapere*, and to align their meanings with the crimes of rape and abduction can only compound various controversies surrounding the crimes. The confusion is not confined to modern critics. Christopher Cannon finds various late fourteenth-century scholars who assert with respective certainty that "raptus necessarily meant abduction and contained no connotation of sexual violence…that rape or forced

[24]The treatises mention different practical considerations that might pertain in respect of different crimes: for example, there might be no immediate suspect on discovery of a murdered body. See *Glanvill*, Book XIV, chapter 3, 174; *Bracton*, II, 350. See also Ibid., 406, 407, 411 for instances when failure properly to instigate the hue and cry in cases of felony might provide grounds to avoid an appeal.

[25]Fletcher and Rowley, *Maid in the Mill*, ed. Bowers, in *The Dramatic Works*, ed., Bowers, 2.2.180, 2.2.214.

[26]Dalton, *Country Justice* (1618), 248.

coitus is the only acceptable translation…[and] that the word *raptus* was so ambiguous…that it could mean either."[27]

Medieval law spans the Statutes of Westminster. Close analysis of its development by medievalists illuminates the background against which terminology and language from pre-conquest and unwritten law adds confusion to statute law. Corrine Saunders traces in detail the complex progress of ancient and early medieval laws of rape and abduction, their European origins and their various linguistic meanings and traditions. She explains that Pre-Conquest Norman law retained elements of Frankish, Gallic, German and Roman traditions. Post-conquest, elements of French feudal law were absorbed into the existing Anglo-Saxon codes; both Anglo-Saxon and early Norman laws distinguished rape and abduction. Common law persisted alongside written law after the Statutes of Westminster. However, under the Normans, women began to lose the legal status they had previously enjoyed—particularly in relation to inheritance. The Anglo-Saxon influence remained throughout the Middle Ages to distinguish English law from Continental European law, although, in the later medieval period, Roman law became more dominant.[28]

Canon law and its commentators defined the word *raptus* specifically in relation to abduction and virginity as the emphasis on marriage and property grew. Saunders gives particularly enlightening insight into how usage of the terms 'rape', '*raptus*' and 'ravishment' evolved from the assimilation of legal traditions, language and culture. She shows its relevance to early medieval law, and in doing so, the basis for confusion over terminology for early modern critics. She describes how the situation is further complicated by the moral and rhetorical arguments arising from theology and canon law. And although overlapping in some respects, canon law and secular law differed in others. Later medieval writers were particularly influenced by *summae*—collections of dogma and commentary. A particular interest in sexuality in the *summae* represented the Church's concern about a matter largely overlooked in secular law. Definitions of rape were proposed in relation to what were perceived to be its various manifestations—"the questions of violence, consent, abduction, status and resistance."[29]

[27] Cannon, "*Raptus*", 75.

[28] Saunders, *Rape and Ravishment*, 27, 30, 119. On medieval rape law, see also Carter, *Rape in Medieval England*; Dunn, *Rape, Abduction, and Adultery*.

[29] Saunders, *Rape and Ravishment*, 76–87, 33–63, 86.an

Contrary to their crucial relevance to the evolution of medieval law, attempts to make either a clear distinction or connection between rape and abduction by means of pre-conquest terminology do not withstand statute law. Saunders's discussion reinforces the point; it also reinforces the suggestion that to propose specific meaning today, for words used inconsistently or ambiguously in early modern texts, is unproductive.

By the 1620s, however, Coke is clear that rape or raptus "is when a man hath carnal knowledge of a woman by force and against her will." Any appeal must contain the word "rapuit", he tells us, for "without this word it cannot be expressed by any periphrasis or circumlocution; for *carnilatur cognovit eam* [he had carnal knowledge of me], or the like, will not serve."[30] The terminology is at the heart of Henry Ansgar Kelly's detailed analysis and interpretation of the statutes which he argues are aimed at abduction, rather than physical violation, throughout, and in which he is particularly critical of Coke. Caroline Dunn is less prescriptive: after close analysis of the language, linguistic devices and recorded cases, she finds that the statutes defy clarity and remain ambiguous.[31]

The temptation to distinguish between rape and ravishment is compounded by reliance on *The Lawes Resolutions*. The author devotes section XXI to "Ravishment in two sorts," but apparently contradicts the notion when he elaborates, saying that only one kind of rape is called "by the common people and by the law itself, Ravishment"—that of rape as sexual violation. He distinguishes, correctly, between rape and abduction, and notes that ravishment is borrowed from the Latin 'rapere' (to seize), "but unproperly, for it is no more but *Species stupri* a hideous hateful kind of whoredome in him which commiteth it": it is rape. Despite the misleading headline, the author makes clear that rape and ravishment are the same crime.[32]

Bracton and Coke, among others, use the words rape and ravishment interchangeably.[33] And in his 1630 edition of *The Country Justice*, Dalton explains that "Ravishment is here taken in one and the same signification with Rape, which is a violent deflowering of a woman, or a Carnall knowledge had of the body of a woman, against her will."[34] Significantly, though

30 Coke, *The First Part*, 123–24.

31 Kelly, "Statutes of Rapes," 361–419, esp. 365, 370, 384–85; Dunn, *Stolen Women*, 31.

32 *Lawes Resolutions*, 377–78.

33 See, for example, Coke, *First Part*, 123, ibid., *The Second Part*, †179, 180, 181; *Bracton*, II, 414–16.

34 Dalton, *Country Justice* (1630), 281.

the rape statutes use the words interchangeably in respect of all types of rape—including elopement and abduction—until the first Abduction Act in 1487. Subsequently, both terms are applied only to felonies prosecuted under the rape statutes: there is no statutory distinction between rape and ravishment.[35] And *neither* term is used in the abduction acts. Instead, the alternatives, "defoulled," "deflower," "violating," and "defiled," describe the personal consequences of a crime primarily against property and inheritance.[36]

It appears that the interchangeable usage of the terms has, at least in part, stimulated an imperative among commentators and critics alike to equate duality in the purpose of the law with a semantic variation. The resulting attention has added further layers to an already confusing subject. However, because misreadings have persisted over a prolonged period, critical expositions are inclined to embrace more than one legal issue. Examples of semantic confusion over the terms rape and ravishment are therefore discussed at the end of Chap. 3, alongside problems of interpretation that emerge in relation to statute law.

Marriage to the Rapist

Bracton describes the origins of medieval provisions that enable a woman to choose to marry her rapist. After reiterating the penalty of loss of eyes and members for rape, the treatise continues:

> Unless…the woman thus defiled claims him for her husband, for this lies wholly in her discretion, not in that of the man, for if it lay in his discretion this unseemliness would result, namely, that a villein or common person might bring perpetual disgrace upon a woman of nobility and good family by a single act of defilement and take her to wife to the disgrace of her family. But suppose the ravisher is a noble man and the woman raped a common person; will it be for the defiled woman to exercise a choice and decide

[35] *Statutes of the Realm*, I (1810), 29, 3 Edward I, the First Statute of Westminster, c. xiii, 1275; Ibid., 87, 13 Edward I, the Second Statute of Westminster, c. xxxiv–xxxv, 1285; Ibid., II (1816), 27, 6 Richard II, c. vi. 1382; Ibid., II, 367, 31 Henry VI, c. ix, 1453; Ibid., II, 512, 3 Henry VII, c. ii, 1487; Ibid., II, 538, 4 Henry VII, c. xiii, 1488–9; Ibid., III (1817), 757, 32 Henry VIII, c. xii, 1540; Ibid., IV, part I, 329 (1819), 4 and 5 Philip and Mary, c. viii, 1557–8; Ibid., 617, 18 Elizabeth I, c. vii, 1575–6; Ibid., IV, part II (1819), 910, 39 Elizabeth I, c. ix, 1597.

[36] Alternatives are used as follows: "defoulled" in the 1487 act, "deflower" and "violating" in the 1557–8 act and "defiled" in the 1597 act.

> whether she will marry a noble man or not…? [T]he choice and the decision will always rest with the woman, for what is a voluntary act on her part will be a necessary act on his, that he may redeem his members…Several maybe accessories, but only one shall be held for the defilement, though the several may be liable for lying with her, for to defile a virgin and to lie with one defiled [are different deeds]. And…it is evident that the same punishment ought not to follow in both cases.[37]

Although the woman's autonomy is recognised as central, the extent of her family's influence on her decision cannot, of course, be known. The wording certainly demonstrates the fundamental importance of status, throughout the institutional structures, by which a woman might be raised by marriage to a social superior, but reduced by marriage to an inferior (whereas a man's financial prospects, rather than his standing, might be the greater priority). Notably, virginity is again crucial: only *its* loss attracts either the full penalty of the law or the alternative of marriage, and subsequent rape by accessories to the original act is regarded as less serious.

Although the premium placed on virginity can be identified throughout medieval and early modern written law, authority for the practice of marriage to the rapist is more tenuous. The dispensation of marriage "nowadays provided," Bracton tells us, "is not by law but by permission of Holy Church and the king. That permission belongs to the king alone within the realm." He relates the myth, originating in France at the beginning of the eleventh century, from which the provision arose, and ends: "This arrangement…grew and became of such high authority that it is now in many places regarded as customary." His words imply the practice was not a general one, and by acknowledging that practice required permission of "Holy Church and the king," he indicates some ambivalence about its authority. Even so, there is little doubt that families continued to facilitate such marriages as a pragmatic alternative to the risk of public shame and loss of marriage prospects associated with an appeal of rape.[38] When reviewing the statutes in early modern times, Coke defined the practice as common law prior to the first Statute of Westminster (Westminster I) of 1275.[39] It might have offered a pragmatic accommodation to prevent disgrace for the woman and her family. But, as will be seen in Chap. 3, it operated in increasing tension with statute law, being

[37] *Bracton*, II, 417.
[38] Ibid., 418, 419.
[39] Coke, *Second Part*, †179–80.

effectively outlawed by the second Statute of Westminster (Westminster II) ten years later in 1285.

But at a time of experimentation on the Jacobean stage, the archaic legal practice provided the playwrights with one of the few viable, non-tragic outcomes for rape. Marriage as a resolution to *The Queen of Corinth* was not the original idea of either Fletcher or his collaborators, Field and Massinger: it originates with the Senecan dilemma of a man who rapes two women. One victim asks for his death and, as allowed in English law before 1285, one victim pleads for his life and to marry him.[40] In *The Queen of Corinth*, there is no dilemma because a bed-trick has been effected to avert tragedy so that Theanor, son of the eponymous Queen, has (conveniently) 'raped' the same woman—his once betrothed, Merione—twice, allowing the ancient law of marriage to the rapist to prevail.[41]

Rape, Conception and Consent

Amongst the common law given in Dalton's 1618 edition of *The Country Justice*, something appears that is notably different from *Bracton*. It is an assumption that "If the woman at the time of the supposed rape, doe conceive with child, by the ravisher, this is no rape, for a woman cannot conceive with child, except she does consent."[42] The assumption, equating conception and consent and therefore precluding rape, can be traced to *Fleta*: "If however, the woman should have conceived at the time alleged in the appeal, it abates, for without a woman's consent she could not conceive."[43] The common law rule was a factor in deciding whether or not statute law had been broken—it was not itself statute law. But *Fleta*'s precept seems to have transmuted into a simple rule which remained extant through the seventeenth and the eighteenth centuries.[44]

The presumption against conception as compatible with rape appears nowhere in *Bracton*, nor does Histed find it mentioned in *The Boke of*

[40] See Coke, *Second Part*, 180.

[41] Fletcher, Field and Massinger, *The Queen of Corinth*, ed. Turner, in *The Dramatic Works*.

[42] Dalton, *Country Justice* (1618), 248.

[43] Histed, "Medieval Rape," 744; Richardson and Sales, *Fleta*, vol. 72, Book II, chapter 33, 89. The discussion of rape and conception in the following paragraphs closely follow Histed's exposition.

[44] Histed, "Medieval Rape" 766–67.

Justices of Peas from 1509 onwards.[45] However, *Britton* confirms and elaborates:

> If the defendant confesses the fact, but says that the woman at the same time conceived by him, and can prove it, then our will is, that it be adjudged no felony, because no woman can conceive if she does not consent.[46]

The *Mirror of Justices* also subscribed to the theory, and through its perpetuation in these treatises, it was established doctrine in early modern common law, continuing to appear throughout subsequent editions of *The Country Justice*. The precept betrays beliefs consistent with the thinking and philosophy of the respective periods, and something that had originated in medical theory and dogma re-emerged as legal rule.[47] It demonstrates a specific evidential difficulty for women bringing rape appeals, reinforcing the historical emphasis for women on reputation and chastity.

Histed meticulously traces the idea from its sources in early Greek philosophy into English legal opinion. It was Hippocrates, in the fifth century B.C., who originally proposed that both men and women produced "seed" which combined at conception. Philosophers agreed "that as women, like men, produced seed, then clearly they must, like men, experience pleasure in the act of intercourse in order for the seed to be emitted and conception to ensue." A century after Hippocrates, Aristotle was among those who argued against the two seed theory on the basis that if the female could produce both seed and environment for it to flourish there was no need for male seed: neither then does the female need to take pleasure in the act. However, adherents of Hippocrates included the physician Galen in the second century, whose ideas were particularly influential in early Western medicine. The debate continued for centuries. To answer the question of how a raped woman could conceive, followers of the two seed theory proposed the distinction between the body and the mind.[48] Writing in the twelfth century, William of Conches argued in his *Dragmaticon*:

[45] Ibid., 759.
[46] *Britton*, ed. Nichols, I, chapter 24, paragraph 7, 114.
[47] Horne, *Mirror of Justices*, chapter III, section 21, 148.
[48] Histed, "Medieval Rape," 745–48.

> Even though the action is displeasing to the raped woman in the beginning, nevertheless due to the weakness of the flesh it pleases in the end…For that which is pleasing to the flesh, is often displeasing to the rational mind.[49]

Copies of the *Dragmaticon* are known to have been available in learned libraries in England in the early thirteenth century. Histed identifies that Christian theology in the language of "weakness of the flesh" and "pleasure 'in the end'" equates with familiar ideas of "temptation of the flesh." However, despite the fact that Conches's discussion is a purely theoretical one on the nature of conception, she notes that as a consequence: "This explanation was soon to be stripped of its context and defined as a simple rule within the English legal system…that conception equated to consent to the act."[50]

Despite renewed interest in Aristotelean philosophy and science in the curricula at Oxford and Paris universities at the beginning of the thirteenth century, it proved impossible to displace the by now well-established Hippocratic and Galenic theory. This was the background against which *Fleta* and *Britton* were written; but the absence of the rule of conception and consent from *The Boke of Justices of Peas*, and the existence of a small number of records of rape and pregnancy indicate acceptance of the rule was not unequivocal.[51]

The few rape appeals involving pregnancy, Histed finds, throw no light on the existence or otherwise of the legal rule, "being either incomplete or mere records of indictment and depositions," with no recorded decision. But she, too, warns that there might be a "simple, and more usual reason" for the lack of records: "that they have not survived the distance of centuries." She is another historian who emphasises that "absence of material gives no conclusive evidence…one way or the other." On the other hand, dozens of cases heard at the church courts in the fifteenth and sixteenth centuries involved moral offences—"fornication, pre-marital sex, adultery, bearing or fathering a bastard, harbouring an illegitimately pregnant woman." Many of the women described acts of enforced sex, suggesting the rule, while not definitive, might have played a part.[52]

[49] Ibid., 750.

[50] Ibid., 750–52 (752).

[51] Ibid., 754; 759–61; Histed describes the case of Lady Butler, an example of rape and pregnancy, see 755–57.

[52] "Medieval Rape," 760, 755; Gowing, *Domestic Dangers: Women Words and Sex in Early Modern England* (Oxford: Clarendon Press, 1998), 31.

The medieval equation of rape and violence, as the extracts from *Bracton* indicate, provided yet another obstacle with which the raped woman had to contend. If visible indications of violence were seen to validate the woman's evidence that the act was against her will, it was a simple step to make the converse assumption that lack of visible injury meant no resistance, which in turn meant consent and no rape.[53] *The Mirror of Justices*, again, appears to subscribe to the belief: of assumed assent:

> because she conceiveth by him at the same time, and there is no presumption that she was ravished against her will by saving of her Garments, nor shedding of blood, nor Hue and Cry made, or other manner of violence offered.[54]

Coke cites the *Mirror of Justices* when specifying force within the definition of rape. And what had started as a mere construct within a theoretical debate about conception became enshrined in legal doctrine.[55]

Hale eventually recorded the authoritative opinion that conception was not a bar to bringing a rape appeal, in his *Historia Placitorum Coronae*.[56] His argument also follows the notion of rape as a yielding, and as such it represents a consent to the act (regardless of menace). He states that consent given in fear or threat of death is "not a consent to excuse rape" and continues: "And therefore…[a woman who has been overcome by force can conceive]." Histed is interested in the presumption created by the word "therefore" that "forced consent" disproves the "'no rape with conception' doctrine", and identifies Hale's thinking as founded in the assumed association of violence with rape. She notes that Hale is not arguing with the apparent belief that rape and conception are legally incompatible, since his opinion still assumes the link between the two, but on the basis of legal theory that a forced consent is a rape.[57] In the absence of statistical evidence, the proportions of recorded and unrecorded rapes resulting in pregnancy are unknown. But when seeking reasons why rape

[53] Histed, "Medieval Rape," 758.

[54] Horne, *Mirror*, 148.

[55] Coke, *First Part of the Institutes*, 123^{v}.

[56] Hale was first called to the bar in 1636. However, the treatise was not published until 1736: see *Oxford Dictionary of National Biography*, s.v. "Hale, Sir Mathew (1609–1676), judge and writer" (by Alan Cromartie), "Major Legal Writings", paragraph 2. https://doi.org/10.1093/ref:odnb/11905, Accessed 6 April 2021.

[57] Histed, "Medieval Rape," 762–65 (762. Histed's translation from the Latin).

seems to be little recorded, the long-established legal doctrine equating conception with consent suggests it might be a factor.

The medieval legal culture incorporated an almost chivalric perception of rape as a crime of lust and an unseemly failure of respect for norms of behaviour prescribed by gender. And, as Histed points out, it places emphasis on the physicality of both evidence and traditions of ordeal and punishment. A man who failed to respect a woman's physical integrity faced a grisly penalty, but a woman faced with rape was responsible for defending herself rigorously against assaults on her person and for providing substantial evidence that she had done so. At the same time, through the statutes, the social and political focus moved from the victim to the wider impact on family and property and the early modern preoccupation with wealth and its acquisition. The statutes themselves, and the circumstances giving rise to them, give an account of the meaning attached to the crime of rape and the importance of its punishment and deterrence from the late thirteenth century to the end of the sixteenth.

Various ancient and early modern legal sources play a part in the discussion of conception and consent. But when they are read against statute law, authoritative commentary or chronology, they can themselves lead to misapprehension about facets of the law. Cynthia Garrett places an emphasis on Dalton which suggests he is responsible for what is, in fact, a reiteration of statute and common law. She finds that "legal handbooks of the period often reinforce the view that female consent may be assumed even when a woman denies." She identifies Dalton's *Country Justice* as seeming "at first sight...to make female consent the decisive factor in determining rape." It apparently does this by "stating that rape occurs if a woman 'doth neither consent before nor after.'" The purpose and contents of this and similar handbooks was precisely an abridgement of existing law, and the statement is a direct quote from Westminster II. It is not a personal "endorsement of the medieval concept of *post facto* consent" by the author. Nor is the provision, as Garrett suggests, linked to ideas of female sexuality exploited by Ovid when he legitimises male force by suggesting a woman "may 'at first' resist but will eventually yield willingly." "Consent...after," as specified in Westminster II, referring to elopement, represents a different matter from that proposed by Ovid: a public decision rather than a private yielding.[58]

[58] Garrett, "Sexual Consent," 41, citing Dalton, *Country Justice* (1618), 247–48: see *Statutes*, I, 87, c. xxxiv.

And yet, to complicate the matter of conception further, the historical record does not suggest sex outside marriage was unusual—reinforced by the inconsistent practices associated with rites of marriage. Martin Ingram comments that "about a fifth of all brides were pregnant by the time they got married in church."[59] This may be unsurprising since, other than among the wealthy or aristocracy, the cost of setting up a household meant the average age for first marriages was about twenty-six or twenty-seven for women, and twenty-eight or twenty-nine for men.[60]

It is not difficult to see how the often confusing business of marriage contracts could easily create the circumstances leading to dispute. In its least complex form, a marriage could be contracted between two people by saying words of the marriage service in the present tense, in the presence of two witnesses (*per verba de praesenti*). The contract was legally binding, although it was usual to solemnise it later in church. In an alternative form, a promise could be made to marry in the future (*per verba de futuro*), but this type of contract could be dissolved by mutual consent. A *conditional* contract was similar: it became binding on the fulfilment of specific conditions such as parental permission or financial settlement. Both types of contract "became immediately and irrevocably binding" if the couple had sexual intercourse and, conversely, both could be superseded if the participants subsequently entered into a *de praesenti* contract with someone else.[61] Consummation was, though, only relevant in relation to legitimising a pre-marriage contract; otherwise, it was consent to the marriage by two people in front of witnesses, not consummation, which made the marriage.[62] However, Ingram tells us that "neither solemnisation in church, nor the use of specially prescribed phrases, nor even the presence of witnesses, was essential to an act of marriage." By the latter part of the seventeenth century, church solemnisation had become customary, but the situation was in flux throughout Elizabeth's reign, and into the early part of the 1600s. Uncertainty about the precise status of the various requirements enabled the continuation of "'clandestine' marriages" which remained a valid formation.[63]

[59] Ingram, *Church Courts*, 157.
[60] Eales, *Women*, 61. See also Ingram, *Church Courts*, 129.
[61] Houlbrooke, "The Making of Marriage", 339–41 (341); Ingram, *Church Courts*, 189–90.
[62] Sommerville, *Sex and Subjection*, 177.
[63] Ingram, *Church Courts*, 132–134 (132, 134).

In addition, ecclesiastical pronouncements and canons lacked clarity on the question of parental consent to marriage, but agreed there should be affection and compatibility between the couple. A full binding commitment could be made at age twelve for women, and fourteen for men.[64] However, there was an overwhelming sense that marriage should only proceed with parental consent up to the age of twenty one (or any age, if by licence).[65]

Houlbrooke observes though that "judges were still ready to uphold contracts, even in the face of opposition from parents and other kinsfolk." His analysis is concerned with the period 1519 to 1563, during which time the trend towards church solemnisation was growing, and pre-church contracts (and therefore litigation) were in decline. On the other hand, Ingram comments, "parental influence in matchmaking was often very strong" and that cases of conflict between parents and children were usually settled in favour of the parents. The apparent disparity in the findings of the two studies might be explained by the different time spans they address. Ingram's study follows on from Houlbrooke's and covers the period from 1570 to 1640, during which time, numbers of cases decline from "a fairly low incidence to the merest trickle." The changing customs and practices over the extended period represent the growing acceptance of church solemnisation as necessary to matrimony, and the decline of marriage contracts—even those confirmed later by a church ceremony. The attitude taken by ecclesiastical judges in contract cases, and in "punishing antenuptial fornication," demonstrates the gradual change.[66]

Disputed marriage also brought with it potential economic consequences. Pregnancy out of wed-lock not only offended as a moral crime, but also as placing a potential burden on the community. Keith Wrightson's study of the Essex village of Terling shows that, during the period 1570–1640, attitudes to bridal pregnancy changed. While some 80% of known bastardy cases were prosecuted, only 40% of cases of bridal pregnancy were brought to the church courts. However, further breakdown shows figures of 35% in 1580–1599 and 28% in 1600–1619, but in 1600–1639, the figure was 73%. Wrightson notes the increasing parallel

[64] Macfarlane, *Marriage and Love in England*, 127; Coke, *Second Part*, 181; Hale, *Historia Placitorum*, 630–31 (numbered 730–31).

[65] Ingram, *Church Courts*, 135–36; Brewer, *By Birth or Consent*, 291–300.

[66] Houlbrooke, "Making of Marriage" 339 (abstract), 341, 340; Ingram, *Church Courts*, 138, 139, 192, 193. For a full discussion of contract cases, see Ingram *Church Courts*, Chapter 6, 189–218, and the reasons for their decline, Chapter 4, 125–167.

between concern with bridal pregnancy and illegitimacy in relation to demographic fluidity and, economic, moral and social considerations.[67]

Various nuances of potential arrangements arise in a sub-plot of *The Maid in the Mill*, the play takes place against the backdrop of revels, darkness, illicit meetings, mistaken identity and secret marriage. Among several allusions to the legalities and breaches caused by the young people marrying against the will of their parents are references to fathers' blessings and powers of prohibition, of the priest and the bedchamber, and unsanctioned marriage as theft.[68]

It is not difficult to see how the business of contracting marriage might give rise to allegations of rape, fornication, coercion or deception. When fallen and abandoned women appear on the stage, it is not always the heroines—the princesses or daughters of dukes—but more often the secondary characters—the lost daughters of generals, lower nobility or lesser sorts—who are coerced, seduced or deceived. The part played by the women is usually pivotal to revealing the hidden nature of male characters, and to resolving the plot. But the equivocal circumstances surrounding their fallen status (and its proximity to rape) allows sympathy rather than condemnation for the woman's situation. As the plot of Philip Massinger's *The Duke of Milan* is resolved, Eugenia tells how, on the strength of Sforza's "hell-deepe oaths" to marry her, she had "given up" her "faire name" and her "mayden honor" to Sforza's "foule lust." In his *The Bashful Lover,* Maria is the exiled general Octavio's estranged daughter, now disguised and cross-dressed as Ascanio his page. She was ruined by Alonzo who now confesses he "hoodwink'd," "besieg" and "took" her "Virgin-fort," "No vows or imprecation forgotten/With speed to marry her." Although his words are not conclusive of rape, they suggest the limits of seduction, if not coercion, facilitated by the ambivalent practices associated with marriage rites.[69]

[67] Wrightson and Levine, *Poverty and Piety*, 127–127. See also Wrightson, *Earthly Necessities: Economic Lives*, 221–226; Ingram, *Carnal Knowledge*.

[68] See, for example, Fletcher and Rowley, *Maid in the Mill*, 4.1.163, 182; 4.3.19–21; 5.1.1–3; 5.2.266–86, 316–17, 344–49.

[69] Massinger, *The Duke of Milan*, in *The Plays and Poems*, ed. Edwards and Gibson, 5.1.45, 46, 47; *The Bashful Lover*, ibid., IV, 4.2.79, 82–84; W.T., Further examples of wronged women are Timandra, in Massinger's *The Bondman*, ibid., I; Bellafront, in Thomas Dekker and Middleton, *The Patient Man and the Honest Whore*, ed. Mulholland, in *The Collected Works*, ed. Taylor and Lavagnino; Anne, in [*Thorney Abbey*, or *The London Maid*, in], *Gratiae theatrales*, ed. Baillie.

Custom, practise and precedent determine common law, and in the case of rape, these engage an amalgam of religious and cultural beliefs about the nature of women—some dating from ancient times. The discussion of the bawdy courts in Chap. 1 makes apparent how attitudes arising from the cultural atmosphere created a moral bind particularly among women from the lower and middle strata of society. When moving on to statute law in the following chapter, it is also clear that written law is more representative of those of wealth, power and influence—in fact those responsible for writing it.

Bibliography

Bowers, Fredson, ed. *The Dramatic Works in the Beaumont and Fletcher Canon*, 10 vols. Cambridge: Cambridge University Press, 1966–1996.

Bracton, Henricus de. *De Legibus et Consuetudinibus Angliae. Bracton*, edited by George E. Woodbine, translated by Samuel E. Thorne. Vol 2. Cambridge, Mass.: Harvard University Press: 1968.

Brewer, Holly. *By Birth or Consent: Children, Law, and the Anglo-American Revolution in Authority*. University of North Carolina Press, 2007.

Britton, edited by F. M. Nichols, 2 vols. Oxford: Clarendon Press, 1865.

Cannon, Christopher. "*Raptus* in the Chaumpaigne Release and a Newly Discovered Document Concerning the Life of Geoffrey Chaucer", *Speculum*, 68 (1993): 74–94.

Carter, John Marshall. *Rape in Medieval England: An Historical and Sociological Study*. Lanham, Md.: University Press of America, 1985.

Coke, Edward. *The First Part of the Institutes of the Laws of England, or a Commentary on Littleton*, 10th edition. London: Rawlins and Roycroft, 1703.

———. *The Second Part of the Institutes of the Lawes of England*. London: Brooke, 1797.

Dalton, Michael. *The countrey justice containing the practice of the justices of the peace out of their sessions*. London: Islip, 1618; 1619; 1622; 1626.

———. *The countrey justice containing the practice of the justices of the peace out of their sessions*. London: Flesher, 1630.

———. *The countrey justice containing the practice of the justices of the peace out of their sessions*. London: Rawlins and Roycroft, 1705.

Davenant, William. *The Unfortunate Lovers: a tragedie*. London: R.H., 1643.

Davenport, Robert (?). *Dick of Devonshire*, edited by G. James, and Mary R. McManaway, The Malone Society vol. 103. British Museum Ms Egerton 1994, folios 30–51; repr. 1955.

Dekker, Thomas, and Thomas Middleton. *The Patient Man and the Honest Whore*, edited by Paul Mulholland, in *Thomas Middleton: The Collected Works*, edited by Gary Taylor and John Lavagnino. Oxford: Oxford University Press, 2010.

Dunn, Caroline. *Stolen Women in Medieval England: Rape, Abduction, and Adultery, 1100–1500*. Cambridge: Cambridge University Press, 2013.

Eales, Jacqueline. *Women in Early Modern England 1500–1700*. London: University College London, 1998.

E[dgar] T[homas]. *The Lawes Resolutions of Womens Rights: Or, The Lawes Provision for Woemen*. London: More, 1632.

Edwards, Philip, and Colin Gibson, eds. *The Plays and Poems of Philip Massinger*, 5 vols. Oxford: Clarendon Press, 1976.

Fleta, edited and translated by H. G. Richardson and G. O. Sayles. Vol. 72. Publications of the Selden Society. London: Selden Society, 1953.

Fletcher, John, Nathan Field, and Philip Massinger. *The Queen of Corinth*, edited by Robert Kean Turner. In Vol. 8 of *The Dramatic Works*, edited by Bowers. 1992.

Fletcher, John, and William Rowley. *The Maid in the Mill*, edited by Fredson Bowers. In Vol. 9 of *The Dramatic Works*, edited by Bowers. 1994.

Garrett, Cynthia E. "Sexual Consent and the Art of Love in the Early Modern English Lyric", *Studies in English Literature, 1500–1900*, 44 (2004): 37–58.

Glanville, Ranulf de. *The Treatise on the Laws and Customs of England Commonly Called Glanvill*, edited by G. D. G. Hall. London: Nelson, in association with the Selden Society, 1965.

Gowing, Laura. *Domestic Dangers: Women Words and Sex in Early Modern London*. 1996. Reprint, Oxford: Clarendon Press, 2005.

Hale, Matthew. *The History of the Common Law in England*, edited by Charles M. Gray. 1713. Reprint, 1739. Reprint, London: University of Chicago Press, 1971.

Hale, Matthew. *Historia Placitorum Coronae*, 2 vols. 1736. Reprint, London: Professional Books, 1971.

Histed, Elise Bennett. "Mediaeval Rape: A Conceivable Defence?", *Cambridge Law Journal*, 63 (2004): 743–69.

Horne, Andrew. *The booke called the mirrour of justices*. London: Walbancke, 1646.

Houlbrooke, Ralph. "The Making of Marriage in Mid-Tudor England: Evidence from the Records of Matrimonial Contract Litigation", *Journal of Family History*, 10 (1985): 339–52.

Ingram, Martin. *Carnal Knowledge: Regulating Sex in England, 1470–1600*. Cambridge: Cambridge, University Press, 2017.

———. *Church Courts, Sex and Marriage in England 1570–1640*. 1987. Reprint, Cambridge: Cambridge University Press, 1994.

Kelly, Henry Ansgar. "Statutes of Rapes and Alleged Ravishers of Wives: A Context for the Charges against Thomas Mallory, Knight". *Viator: Medieval and Renaissance Studies* 28 (1997): 361–419.

Law, Jonathan. editor, *Dictionary of Law, A*, 9th edition. Oxford: Oxford University Press, 2018.

Macfarlane, Alan. *Marriage and Love in England: Modes of Reproduction 1300–1840*. Oxford: Blackwell, 1986.

A Manuall or analecta... formerly styled The complete justice. London: Flesher, 1641.

Massinger, Philip. *The Bashful Lover*. In Vol. 4 of *The Plays and Poems*, edited by Edwards and Gibson. 1976.

———. *The Bondman*. In Vol. 1 of *The Plays and Poems*, edited by Edwards and Gibson. 1976.

———. *The Duke of Milan*. In Vol. 1 of *The Plays and Poems*, edited by Edwards and Gibson. 1976.

———. *The Unnatural Combat*. In Vol. 2 of *The Plays and Poems*, edited by Edwards and Gibson. 1976.

Peele, George. *The Love of King David and Fair Bethsabe*, London: Islip, 1599. Reprint, edited by W.W. Greg. Malone Society, 1907.

Post, J. B. "Ravishment of Women and the Statutes of Westminster", in *Legal Records and the Historian: Papers Presented to the Cambridge Legal History Conference, 7–10 July 1975*, edited by J. H. Baker, 150–164. London: Royal Historical Society, 1978.

Saunders, Corrine J. *Rape and Ravishment in the Literature of Medieval England*. Cambridge: Brewer, 2001.

Solga, Kim. "*Violence Against Women in Early Modern Performance: Invisible Acts*". Basingstoke: McMillan, 2009.

Statutes of the Realm, 12 vols. London: England Record Commission, 1810–1828.

Toner, Barbara. *The Facts of Rape*. London: Arrow, 1977.

W. T. [*Thorney Abbey*, or *The London Maid*, in], *Gratiae theatrales, or, A choice ternary of English plays composed upon especial occasions by several ingenious persons*. London: R.D., 1662.

Wilson, Arthur. *The Swisser*, edited by Linda V. Itzoe, The Renaissance Imagination series, 7. London: Garland, 1984.

Wrightson, Keith. *Earthly Necessities: Economic Lives in Early Modern Britain*. New Haven Conn.; London: Yale University Press, 2000.

———. *Poverty and Piety in an English Village: Terling, 1525–1700*. Oxford: Clarendon, 1995.

CHAPTER 3

Statute Law

Abstract This chapter sets out the statutes of rape elopement and abduction, and identifies the main areas of contention that surround the subject. From the thirteenth century to the present, interpretation of rape law in early modern England has been controversial among legal professionals—and therefore confusing for the non-specialist. The question of whether the statutes of Westminster (1275 and 1285) were primarily aimed at physical rape or abduction remains, and questions of consent, and of consent after, add to the mix. A 1487 act under Henry VII introduced an abduction act—effectively creating a separate sequence. The medieval statutes also marked the beginning of a shift from prosecution by private appeal to crown indictment. But although women were regarded as inferior beings in an era which privileged the interests of the crown, community and family over the individual, it is a mistake to interpret rape law from a modern perspective of female autonomy. A historical context allows a more nuanced picture than straightforward patriarchy and victimhood. While aristocratic women were subject to the politics of marriage and widowhood, they were active in forging family and political alliances, trading in wardships and defending their inheritances through the offices of the crown.

Keywords Rape • Elopement and abduction • Statutes of rape • Abduction act • Marriage to the rapist • Age of consent • Wardship

H. Barker, *Rape in Early Modern England*,
https://doi.org/10.1007/978-3-030-82609-3_3

Written rape law remained unchanged from Elizabethan times until the death penalty for the crime was repealed in 1840.[1] The statutes were introduced over a three-hundred-year period, from the end of the thirteenth century to the sixteenth, progressively complicating the law and attracting differing legal interpretation and opinions in their own time and in the present. The purpose in this chapter is to set out a concise overview of the relevant statutes, to identify areas of controversy, and to draw attention to sources of detailed analysis and insight. It is clear, when lawyers have disagreed over centuries, that it is dangerous for the non-specialist critic to assume the statutes provide a clear and definitive meaning either individually or as a sequence. Statutory rape law extant in early modern England encompassed the various social, financial and sexual possibilities implicit in a woman's removal from her family. It developed from medieval times when rape had also come to include elopement and abduction—each potentially causing a loss of marriage prospects and consequent disadvantage to the family. From the early inception of the written law and into the seventeenth century, attempts in both law and commentary to define and redefine the offences of rape and abduction militate against clarity. And instances of poor drafting throughout the statutes contribute to obscure the meaning of various clauses. It can hardly be surprising that the interpretation of these laws has been fraught with confusion.

Today it is easy to view the evolving medieval and early modern rape law, with its emphasis on a woman's marriage value, as enabling women's autonomy to be subsumed to misogynistic concern for power and wealth. However, in historical terms, the law represents a tension between the importance of females to the dynastic and material fortunes of the family, and their personal welfare. But, as well as fundamental questions of interpretation and the balance between a woman's welfare and her material value, there were other competing pressures which, at different times, influenced the introduction or drafting of legislation while often adding complexity. For instance, public order was bound up with the reputation of the crown. The law offered a means by which to demonstrate intent at critical political moments, while the exertion of control over public order, crime and punishment increasingly enabled the king or queen to reinforce the legitimacy of monarchy. At the same time, the law offered the sovereign an opportunity to raise revenue by substituting fines for capital punishment, or by taking up a suit if the victim or her family failed to

[1] Toner, *Facts of Rape*, p. 98.

pursue it. Discussion of the statutes will identify four examples where it is known or suspected that a statute was written or amended in response to a single high-profile incident.

Several statutes address rape among other felonies. Rather than viewing rape law in isolation, which inevitably places an emphasis on the question of gender, it is helpful to look at the crime in relation to another capital felony. In her monograph on murder, K. J. Kesselring notes that "the story of medieval law" has been described as "the growth of 'the king's peace'."[2] As the statutes progress, they show a marked shift away from private appeal to prosecution at the king's suit. In ancient times, both murder and rape were regarded as crimes committed against the person or their kin—rather than against the king—and liable to compensation, or otherwise the risk of feuding and violent revenge. While, by the late twelfth century, all homicides came within the scope of the king's peace, the distinction between murder and manslaughter (simple homicide) remained. In medieval law, both were felonies, but "excusable killings" might be acquitted or pardoned; however, by early modern times, killing was seen as an offence against the king.[3] As later discussion will show, avoidance of punishment for both rape and murder (along with other felonies) via sanctuary, pardons and benefit of clergy (claimed by recital of a verse from the Bible) were limited or removed by late fifteenth- and early sixteenth-century statutes. The appeal gradually became viewed as a means of circumventing the legal process and "derided" by association with the feud.[4] Despite persisting to some extent, by the end of the seventeenth century, the private complaint was regarded as little more than an anachronism that lacked the legitimacy of public justice. At the same time, the king's peace was increasingly perceived in terms of "'the public peace' and 'public justice'," while fines and forfeiture benefitted the crown rather than the victim.[5] It is clear that murder and rape—among other felonies—separately or collectively, follow a similar pattern of historical movement. The pattern is not simply driven by the gendered beliefs embedded in the religion, learning and social structures but in the unfolding progress from private, to crown, to public justice.

[2] Kesselring, *Making Murder Public*, 18.

[3] Ibid., 20, 3; on excusable killings and pardons, see 20, note 62.

[4] Ibid., 35

[5] Ibid., 90, 36, 70 (36). But see also Kesselring, "Felony Forfeiture": forfeiture of a felons goods acted as a deterrent, but those other than the crown came to profit from the practice (275,276).

Rape, Elopement and Abduction

Two statutes are commonly associated with the beginning of the written law against rape: the First Statute of Westminster (Westminster I), 1275 and the Second Statute of Westminster (Westminster II), 1285. The two statutes were amended or consolidated by a further nine, encompassing rape, elopement and abduction. The last of these statutes was introduced under Elizabeth I in 1597. However, in 1487, Henry VII introduced, "An Act against taking away of Women against theire Will," seemingly treating abduction as separate from rape and elopement. Abduction, B. J. and Mary Sokol explain, "defined the offences of forcibly taking away women who had, or were heirs to, property"—in effect the theft of a woman.[6] Flexibility between the two sequences remained: elopement, like abduction, had serious implications for lineage, inheritance and property and could be pursued under either rape or abduction law.[7] However, the act added to the existing lack of clarity and has subsequently added to the debate about the interpretation of the statutes.

Although legal professionals from the thirteenth century to the present have accepted the two Westminster statutes as dealing with physical rape, not all agree. Henry Ansgar Kelly argues that the law against rape dates from the earlier Statute of Merton—an act against the ravishment of a ward.[8] By a close attention to the texts, and analysis of language and cases, Kelly links the Merton statute directly to the property elements of the Westminster statutes. He argues, against J.B Post (and also against Sir Edward Coke) that sexual violation was secondary to the abduction and property provisions of Westminster I and II, and remained the primary focus throughout the statutes. Physical rape, he argues, was identified in *Statutes*, under the separate heading "The Office of the Coroner," located directly after Westminster I. It neither defines nor identifies a penalty for

[6] Sokol, *Shakespeare, Law, and Marriage*, 108–109 (108).

[7] The rape statutes: *Statutes of the Realm*, I (1810), 29, 3 Edward I, the First Statute of Westminster, c. xiii, 1275; Ibid., 87, 13 Edward I, the Second Statute of Westminster, c. xxxiv–xxxv, 1285; Ibid., II (1816), 27, 6 Richard II, c. vi, 1382; Ibid., 367, 31 Henry VI, c. ix, 1453; Ibid., 538, 4 Henry VII, c. xiii, 1488; Ibid., III (1817), 757, 32 Henry VIII, c. xii, 1540; Ibid., IV, part I, 617, 18 Elizabeth I, c. vii, 1575–6. The abduction statutes: *Statutes*, II, 512, 3 Henry VII, c. ii, 1487; Ibid., IV, part I, 329 (1819), 4 & 5 Philip and Mary, c. viii, 1557–8; Ibid., IV, part II (1819), 910, 39 Elizabeth I, c. ix, 1597.

[8] *Statutes*, I, 20 Henry III, c. vi, 1235. Kelly, "Statutes of Rapes," 366; see 365, and 384 for Kelly's refutation of the tradition of recognising Westminster I and II as dealing with physical rape.

the crime. It simply states the duties and evidence required by the coroner (similarly to that described in *Bracton*, bloodied wounds, hue and cry) in the case of an appeal of rape. However, if, as Kelly argues, both Merton and the Westminster statutes are concerned with abduction, not physical rape, it is not clear under what statute action is pursued in the light of the coroner's investigation.[9]

Differences in reading the statutes in relation to rape (as a physical violation), or abduction, or both, is a central question of debate. The purpose in this chapter is less to offer interpretations than to set out the statutes succinctly and in order, drawing attention to some of the controversies that beset the subject. The progression of statutes represents variations to the definitions and penalties attached to the crimes, and therefore to their perceived importance. No single rape statute can be taken to represent 'the law' at any particular moment. As Sir Matthew Hale's explanation of the beginning of written law and its relationship with common law suggests (see Chap. 2), each statute obtains its meaning only in the context of the common law and in relation to existing legislation: in other words, whether it adds to, amends or supersedes part, or all, of the existing written law.

The Preface to Westminster I, made at the first parliament held by Edward I after his coronation, makes it clear that the act represented a reaction by the king to the state of law and order, and moral authority in the country:

> Because the State of the Holy Church had been evil kept, and...the Peace less kept, and the Laws less used, and the Offenders less punished, than they ought to be, by reason whereof the People [of the Land] feared less to offend.[10]

Rape is the subject of one brief chapter within an extensive statute. A combination of Latin and Anglo-French terms in the drafting of the statute has created ambiguity and controversy that remains into present times; scholars have variously interpreted it as aimed solely at abduction, or at rape—in the modern sense of sexual violation—or both.[11] The chapter concerns the taking or ravishing of under-age (twelve-year-old) females regardless of

[9] Kelly, "Statutes of Rapes," 367; *Statutes*, I, 40, IV Edward IV, The Office of the Coroner, 1275–1276; *Bracton*, ed. Woodbine, trans. Thorne, II, 415.

[10] *Statutes*, I, 29, c. xiii, 1275.

[11] See, Kelly, "Statutes of Rapes," 366; Dunn, *Stolen Women*, 30, 33, 35–37.

consent, and over-age or married women without consent. The penalty was two years imprisonment and a fine.[12]

> And the King prohibiteth that none do ravish, nor take away by force, any Maiden within Age, neither by her own consent, nor without; nor any Wife or maiden of full Age, nor any other Woman against her Will; and if any so do, at his Suit that will sue within forty days, the King shall do common right; and if none commence his suit within Forty Days, the King shall sue; and such as be found culpable, shall have Two Years Imprisonment, and after shall fine at the King's Pleasure; and if they have not whereof, they shall be punished by longer Imprisonment, according as the Trespass requireth.[13]

Westminster I extends the ancient law of rape from virgins to include matrons, and introduces a rule which states that an appeal of rape must be brought within forty days. The rule is still found in late seventeenth-century treatises although it is omitted from Dalton's *Country Justice* prior to the 1626 edition (see Chap. 2).[14] Failure to appeal speedily, Post suggests, was taken as "tacit consent." He speculates on the imprecision of the term "common right" should the victim bring the suit within forty days.[15] He finds the statute unclear, and could be taken to imply that in such cases some more severe punishment, such as mutilation under the earlier law, might still be considered, although he regards it as unlikely. However, this is precisely the meaning assumed by Hale if at "the suit of the party" concerned, and "if commenced within forty days."[16] The statute does not say that the woman cannot sue after forty days: if, as Hale suggests, a limit was discretionary, it is possible that the woman might still bring an appeal with a view to financial recompense while the king would bring an indictment through his Attorney General. However, contrary to Kelly, by close linguistic analysis and relevant case law, Caroline Dunn argues that the statute did not, indeed, remove a woman's existing right to pursue an appeal—in which circumstances the crime remained a felony.

[12] On twelve as the age of consent, see Coke, *The Second*, 181. However, under subsequent statutes, the question becomes controversial. The arguments are discussed in relation to the relevant statutes, below.

[13] *Statutes*, I, 29, c. xiii, 1275.

[14] Dalton, *The countrey justice*, various edns (1618–1626).

[15] Post, "Ravishment of Women," ed. Baker, 158, 151. On ancient law see *Bracton*, ed. Woodbine, trans. Thorne, II, 414–15, and Chap. 2.

[16] Hale, *Historia Placitorum Coronae*, I, 627.

But should the victim not appeal within forty days, the statute enabled the Crown to prosecute the crime as a trespass, and to levy a fine.[17]

The possibility of prosecution at the king's suit added pressure to the choices available to a victim: whether she should pursue an appeal which she would otherwise have chosen to suppress, whether she or her family colluded in an accommodation with her abductor and/or rapist, or whether she risked the slur of consent should the crown sue in her stead. But regardless of who sued, Post tells us that conviction contributed to a "developing fashion for buying pardons of Crown suit." Despite the stated intention of Westminster I to restore public order, the effect on rape was, seemingly, to produce negligible improvement. Cases rarely reached a proper conclusion: a pattern "of increasingly meticulous exceptions to increasingly circumstantial appeal" developed. The contribution to this state of affairs made by judges might be attributed either to an attitude of male "conservatism" or to a wish to help facilitate the increasing trend for the crown to levy fines and sell pardons. At the same time, the victim became the object of increased moral scrutiny.[18]

Unremarked in the records is the matter of conception. Despite the presumption against rape where the victim conceives, it is unlikely that a consequent pregnancy would be apparent in so short a time. Elise Bennett Histed allows for the possibility that it influenced reporting of the crime—but with caution; Miranda Chaytor is "not convinced" that the doctrine of conception can account for underreporting. However, her argument is substantially based on her doubt that many women or rural justices of the peace were aware of the rule.[19] The legal reputation of Dalton and the influence and regular reprints of his *Country Justice*, together with the circulation of innumerable advisory treatises for the benefit of justices (with or without formal legal training), and the regular output of statutes, might suggest otherwise.[20] But also, in view of Hale's indication that by

[17] Hale, *Historia Placitorum Coronae*, I, 633; Dunn, *Stolen Women*, 29–42, esp. 36–37.

[18] Post, "Ravishment of Women," 155.

[19] Histed, "Mediaeval Rape," 754–55, and 759–60; Chaytor, "Husband(ry): Narratives of Rape", 403–404, note 14.

[20] On the widespread use of *The Country Justice*, see *Oxford Dictionary of National Biography*, s.v. "Dalton, Michael (1564–1644), barrister and legal writer" (by D. A. Orr), paragraph 3. https://doi.org/10.1093/ref:odnb/7067. Accessed 6 April 2021. The numerous editions of Dalton's *Country Justice* and treatises for justices of the peace by Lambarde and Fitzherbert are identified in Chap. 2. The *STC* catalogues over three hundred

early modern times the time limit was discretionary, the possibility of its limited effect remains.[21]

But the forty-day rule has significance in another important respect. The introduction of the king's suit is symptomatic of the shifting emphasis of the law, away from private prosecution, to the Crown. With increasing association of the appeal, generally, with revenge, compensation, or private feuds, Post suggests, that failure to appeal speedily in the case of rape was taken as an indication of malicious prosecution.[22] When Hale gave his opinion towards the end of the seventeenth century, it was that "a year and a day is not allowd in this appeal, but some short time, tho it be not defined in law what time, but lies much in the discretion of the court upon the circumstances of the fact." Although vague in relation to rape, Hale is presumably drawing a comparison with other crimes, but not murder: the king's suit was privileged over that of the victim's family by the same 1487 statute that allowed abduction to be pursued separately from rape.[23]

The effect of Westminster I had been to blur the distinction between rape and abduction. Post tells us that "[t]he terms of Westminster II" make it clear "that Westminster I, c.13, was considered wholly inadequate."[24] Certainly it laid the foundation for controversy that has persisted into the present, and which Westminster II did little to diminish. The first, capital, clause of Westminster II is anomalous, as a French passage in an otherwise Latin text:

> if a Man…do ravish a Woman, married, Maid, or other, where she did not consent, neither before nor after, he shall have Judgement of Life and of Member. And likewise where a Man ravisheth a Women, married Lady, Damosel, or other, with Force, although she consent after, he shall have such Judgement as before said, if he be attainted at the King's Suit, and there the King shall have the Suit.[25]

items between 1560 and 1660 that either commend themselves, or notify statutory obligations or decisions of cases, to justices.

[21] On conception as a defence, see also Baker, *Oxford History*, 563.

[22] Post, "Ravishment of Women," 153.

[23] Hale, *Historia Placitorum Coronae*, I, 633; Kesselring, *Making Murder Public*, 68.

[24] Post, "Ravishment of Women", 156.

[25] *Statutes*, I, 87, c. xxxiv–xxxv, 1285.

If the intention was to make felonies of rape, abduction and elopement, Westminster II ostensibly made them all capital offences and, as a result, elevated the property interests in a way that did not necessarily suit the injured parties. Further confusion arose from the statute's failure to mention the age at which consent became relevant, allowing offences against girls under age to continue to be treated as a misdemeanour under Westminster I.[26] But nor was it just the capital clause which might have caused families to seek alternative remedies. The Latin text continues:

> And of Women carried away with the Goods of their Husbands, the King shall have the Suit for the Goods so taken away. And if a Wife willingly leave her Husband, and go away, and continue with her Advouterer, she shall be barred for ever of Action to demand her Dower...

Here again, a successful felony suit meant any restitution would be lost as forfeiture to the crown. The often mutual will of the injured party and offender to avoid the statutory legislation allowed the exploitation of which Post offers several examples.[27]

After close analysis, Dunn finds the French text ambiguous, leaving a question as to whether the authors intended to legislate against either or both rape and abduction, whether, indeed, they left the statute "deliberately ambiguous." However, she suggests the situation is clearer when it is understood that both statutes allow the crime to be treated as either a felony (if the woman complains), or a trespass in the case of abduction and private settlements (under the king's suit). And, notably the effect of the rape chapters of the Westminster legislation is to make clear the king's interest in upholding the law and in profiting from fines and forfeitures.[28]

While, historically, the statute has been interpreted by legal professionals as specifically concerning sexual rape, Kelly is clear that the Westminster statutes were primarily aimed at abduction "and only secondarily, or not at all, with sexual violation."[29] Post believes the capital clause was "almost certainly an afterthought," arising from a verbal addendum after a single case of rape came before the king "on the first day of the parliament which enacted the statute." He finds that the statute was "sloppily drafted" and

[26] The age of consent is discussed below, in relation to the 1575–6 statute.
[27] Post, "Ravishment of Women," 159–60.
[28] Dunn, *Stolen Women*, 31, 36–37.
[29] Kelly, "Statutes of Rapes," 365–66 (366).

is confident it was actually "aimed at the material and familial aspects of a consenting illicit relationship."[30]

Particularly significant is the wording that a woman consents "neither before nor after." Post suggests that it meant "the time-honoured concord by marriage [to which 'consent after' is implicit] was removed" by the statute. In such cases, for the sake of the woman's reputation, marriage was obviously preferable to the imposition of the capital penalty leaving a woman (and any resulting progeny) without support and in an invidious position to find another suitor. Nor did a family want their prospective damages to go to the crown "as forfeitures for felony." It might then be unsurprising that Post's research shows that "[l]itigants subsequently went to some trouble to circumvent [the] implications" of Westminster II. The threat of resorting to the law presumably placed disgruntled parents or guardians in a strong position to bargain for recompense. Of course, the extent to which the woman herself sanctioned any such arrangement cannot be known.[31]

However, the practice of marriage to the rapist increasingly had become suspected of facilitating marriage between a woman and her suitor against the wishes of one or other's family. For the sake of her reputation, a woman could not admit to having consented to pre-marital sex. By consenting retrospectively, she could both protect her reputation and hope to force her family to accept the man of her choice. Since Westminster I, the notion of "consent after" had been bound up with the interests of the crown. Now under Westminster II, via the King's Suit, the family, too, could override the wishes of the woman who wished to marry the rapist after the event. But Dunn warns against assuming the phrase 'consent after' is to disadvantage eloping women: she points out that it protects a victim against pressure or coercion after the event.[32]

Just as women were aware of the law's potential to facilitate marriage by forcing the hands of their families, they might also have been aware of its potential to put pressure on reluctant lovers. The impossibility of ascribing patterns of behaviour to limited evidence must be reiterated, but before Westminster II, Post finds a "disparity of status…apparent in many cases" in which he discerns "the classic and hopeless plight" of "ruined

[30] Post, "Ravishment of Women," 156, 157. Westminster II is the first instance of four over the ensuing three hundred years which commentators or historians attribute statutory changes to specific, single incidents of rape coming to the attention of the crown.

[31] Post, "Ravishment of Women," 158,159, 157.

[32] Dunn, *Stolen Women*, 40–41.

peasants" and "discarded mistresses" seeking "to salvage honour if not revenge from a social superior." Whatever degree of coercion was involved in these ostensibly consensual cases, a more generalised male fear and suspicion of exploitation by disenchanted women might well have contributed to a reluctance to convict men for rape.[33]

By subsuming rape, in the sense of sexual violation, to its economic meanings of abduction and elopement, Westminster I and II between them effectively created a capital felony of sexual relations outside wedlock. Post explains how this contributed to the muddle and ambiguity over the term 'ravishment', which had always been used in relation to "forcible coition." Although, through Westminster, II the term clearly defined rape, elopement and abduction within the felony clause, it did not eventually prevent confusion between plaintiffs and judiciary on the question of to whom a plea fell—the parent or guardian, or the woman—and whether it should be one of trespass or ravishment. While Kelly's semantic analysis adds yet another level of complexity to the vexed debate about the terms 'rape' and 'ravishment', Post and Kelly coincide in the view that Westminster II, in practice, had more impact on material loss than a woman's sexual violation. Post describes it as "a unique paradox which was never satisfactorily resolved." He concludes that the Statutes ofWestminster "failed to affect [sexual] behaviour." Rather they "inhibited the purposes of the woman herself...and fostered the interests of those who wanted material recompense for the material disparagement wrought by self-willed womenfolk and suitors."[34] In the case of "allegedly kidnapped" wives, according to Kelly, "most case...were walkouts and runaways, who usually had good cause to be shut of their husbands."[35] However, Dunn warns that Post overstates the apparent lack of sympathy implied by the conflation of rape and abduction, and the Crown's suit. She reminds us that a woman retained her right of appeal; that "the royal policy of curbing private settlements in favour of the king's suit was not initiated by the Westminster legislation and not limited to rape cases." In addition, the decline in rape cases began earlier than the Westminster statutes. Even so, she acknowledges that whereas appeals predominated to the end of the

[33] Post, "Ravishment of Women", 152. Post lists some dozen or so cases from various court records from the early thirteenth century.

[34] Ibid., 159, 160; Kelly, "Statutes of Rapes," 366 and *passim*.

[35] Prior to the Statutes of Westminster, Post, "Ravishment of Women," 152, finds more evidence of marriage to the rapist than of straightforward financial settlement; Kelly, "Statutes of Rapes," 363.

thirteenth century, prosecution was increasingly by indictment from the turn of the fourteenth.[36] Post finds only one recorded case attracting the full sentence. Even in that instance, the convict was allowed "to make fine for life and limb" (to pay a fine in lieu of statutory punishment). Evidence of its negligible use suggests the clause was an ill-considered reaction to the event which inspired it. Whatever the intentions behind Westminster II, its drafting allowed inconsistency and confusion in its wake. Subsequent statutes were then destined to compound the lack of clarity.

Despite the capital provisions of Westminster II, according to Post, elopement and abduction "remained far from uncommon" in the fourteenth century.[37] Almost a century later, a further statute, 6 Richard II, chapter 6 (1382), was introduced. It refers to "Offenders and Ravishers…in these Days offending more violently, and much more than they were wont." Although it specifically aligns elopement with rape, it is exclusively concerned with property and inheritance. It offered protection to "Ladies, and the Daughters of Noblemen, and other Women, in every Part of the said Realm." The inclusion of "other women" does not disguise the reality that it is only realistically relevant to those of means, and it further relegates the interests of the women themselves. It continues:

> Wheresoever and whensoever such Ladies', Daughters, and other Women aforesaid be ravished, and after such Rape do consent to such Ravishers, that as well as the Ravishers, as they that be ravished, and every of them, be from henceforth disabled, and by the same Deed be unable to have or challenge all Inheritance, Dower, or Joint Foeffment after the Death of their Husbands and Ancestors.

It goes on to provide that eloping couples should be treated as dead for inheritance purposes, so completing the "extension of legal wrong" to the woman's family. Critically for eloping women, the statute allowed appeals to be brought by fathers, husbands and next of kin. Dunn explains that only after this statute were women who consented to an abductor at any time, disadvantaged.[38]

Bearing in mind that at this time judgment might be determined by combat, it also contained a further clause:

[36] Dunn, *Stolen Women*, 40, 80; Post, "Ravishment of Women," 157.
[37] Post, "Sir Thomas West," 25.
[38] *Statutes*, II, 27, c vi, 1382; Post, "Sir Thomas West," 25; Dunn, *Stolen Women*, 41.

> And...the Husbands...or...the Fathers or other next of their Blood, have from henceforth the Suit to pursue, and may sue against the same Offenders and Ravishers in this Behalf, and to have then thereof convict of Life, and Member, although the same Women after such Rape do consent to the said Ravishers. And further it is accorded, That the Defendant in this Case shall not be received to wage Battle, but that the Truth of the Matter be thereof tried by Inquisition of the Country.

The clause ensured the protection of the family so that elderly fathers, for example, were not potentially obliged to fight judicial duels against young suitors or sons-in-law, while tightening the families' control in relation to marriage and inheritance. The provision is acknowledged in Robert Davenport's play, *Dick of Devonshire*, when Don Fernando, the raped Eleanora's father, remarks that "the Law yet weares a sword in our defence," alluding to trial by combat. But later, when the innocent Manuell seeks trial by combat on another count, the Duke reminds him that the law takes account of potential inequity: "Say he that does accuse | should be decrepitt, lame and weake, or sickly | the other strong and lusty," the law says that when important matters are at stake—like patricide—"you then must call the law into the field,| but not the man."[39]

Similarly to Westminster II, the catalyst for the introduction of the 1382 statute appears to have been a single case: the abduction of Sir Thomas West's daughter Eleanor by one of his retinue, Nicholas Clifton. West obtained a commission for the arrest of Clifton. Although no action seems to have been pursued, Clifton obtained a pardon, and despite an "indictment alleging that he and his friends 'treasonably rose against the king and his people'," that too seems to have fallen by the wayside. It seems that the abduction, already a felony under Westminster II, became treasonable by virtue of its proximity to the royal circle, presumably threatening the political order and destabilising relationships close to the king. At the next parliament, the statute was passed. West claimed credit for it, but although he rightly suspected Eleanor had married Clifton, he was unsuccessful in his attempt to have it made retrospective.[40]

The West incident sharply illustrates the seriousness and priority attached to the issues of property, wealth and political alliance that

[39] Davenport [?], *Dick of Devonshire*, ed. McManaway and McManaway, 3.4.14, 5.1.133–135, and 138–139.

[40] Post, "Sir Thomas West," 25–26 (26). In his paper, Post gives a detailed account of the circumstances surrounding the case, as well as its ramifications.

coalesced around the definition and law of rape. An acknowledgement in the 1382 statute of the frequency and violence of the offence suggests the West affair as being the catalyst to deal with a more extensive problem. The provisions of Westminster II had presumably proved either too ambiguous or too easy to circumvent to have given West the satisfaction he demanded—though he was not able to apply the new statute to his case. Despite these inauspicious beginnings, an apparently successful marriage ensued since Clifton's mother-in-law, Alice, left the couple a "considerable proportion" of her wealth in her will.[41] It is perhaps salutary that, had her father had his way, Eleanor would have been disinherited and Clifton executed in the cause of West's aspirations for status and wealth.

In a 1390 statute, the King excluded those who commit murder with malice aforethought, treason and rape, from "Charters of Pardon…to nourish the more Quietness and Peace within his Realm." Notably, rape is recognised among the most serious felonies.[42]

As the rights to prosecute for elopement, abduction and rape transferred to families, so those wishing to exploit them became more inventive. Henry VI's 1453 statute was concerned with bonds entered into under duress by victims of abduction.[43] Abduction without sexual violation remained outside the definitions of felony, and if a victim was forced to sign away wealth or agree to marriage the bond was "good in law." The 1453 statute did not outlaw abduction, but provided for such bonds to be voided.[44]

In 1487, Henry VII introduced the act that is crucial to modern readings of the statutes: the first abduction act that apparently separated abduction from rape and elopement and began a separate sequence.[45] It was followed by a further two acts. Discussion of the 1487 and subsequent abduction acts follows the review of rape statutes below. In the meantime, refinement to the law of rape and elopement continued.

[41] Ibid., 28–29 (29).

[42] *Statutes*, II, 13 Richard II, Statute 2, c. 1.

[43] Ibid., II, 367, c. ix, 1453.

[44] Ives, "'Agaynst taking'," 24.

[45] *Statutes*, II, 512, c. ii, 1487.

Rape and Elopement After 1487

Of the remaining three statutes in the rape and elopement sequence, none concerned rape and elopement alone: all included rape as one felony alongside others. Until the late fifteenth century, rape, as a felony, was a clergyable offence. This meant that a convicted offender who was a clergyman, or able to read a verse from a prayer book, or more usually from the Bible, could claim benefit of clergy and escape capital punishment. (The first lines of psalm 51 became known as the 'neck verse': "Have mercy on me, O God, according to your steadfast love; according to your abundant mercy blot out my transgressions").[46] Felons with either an education or the wit to memorise the text were therefore at liberty to repeat their crimes. In "An Act to take awaye the benefytt of Clergy from certayne persons," the statute 4 Henry VII, c. 13, 1488 stipulated that because of continual abuse among those "more bold to commit murdre rape robbery thefte and all other myschievous dedys," clergy could only be claimed once. The offender would be branded with a letter T on his thumb to avoid an offender making a second claim.[47] Henry VIII then abolished sanctuary as a means for those who commit "Murder, Rape, Burglary, Robbery, Arson, Sacrilege; or their Accessories" to evade the law, in 32 Henry VIII, chapter 12 (1540).[48] Murder was included alongside rape in both of these statutes.

In 1575–6, in the final statute relevant to the rape/elopement sequence, Elizabeth I removed benefit of clergy from a first offence. Rape was encompassed in the act because of its status as a felony rather than being its sole objective, and the preamble employs rhetoric consistent with the intention to impose order and the authority of the crown—the Queen's peace. But significantly, although murder was recognised as the most heinous crime ahead of rape, it is not included in this statute, and clergy was still apparently an accepted plea in the late seventeenth and eighteenth centuries.[49] The statute stated its objective as "the repressinge of the moste wicked and felonious Rapes or Ravishments...and of felonious Burglaries, and for the avoydinge of sundrye Perjuries and other Abuses in and aboute

[46] On benefit of clergy, see Sokol, *Shakespeare, Law, and Marriage*, 108, 165, 225, note 9; Sharpe, 95; although Sharpe incorrectly states that "rape never came within the scope of clergy."

[47] *Statutes*, II, 538, c. xiii, 1488.

[48] Ibid., III, 757 (marginal heading).

[49] See Kesselring, *Making Murder Public*, 91, 152.

the purgacion of Clerkes convicte."[50] It does not support arguments for a significant change either in the legal relationship to abduction or in attitudes to rape. However, a separate, fourth clause states:

> Yf any person shall unlawfully and carnally knowe and abuse any Woman Childe under the Age of Tenne yeeres, everie suche unlawful and carnall knowledge shall be Fellonye, and the Offender thereof being dewlye convicted shall suffer as a Felon without Alleauwance of Clergie.[51]

A footnote to the clause tells us that it is "annexed to the Original Act in a separate Schedule." Its late inclusion supports the assumption that this was yet another example of a reaction to a particular case that came to the attention of the Queen. Coke cites the incident as material to the amendment. According to *the Lawes Resolutions*, the clause arose after a child of six was raped by a "Scot." The case did not proceed to judgment because of a legal anomaly.[52] Prior to Elizabeth's 1575–6 statute, Hale tells us: "It was doubted whether rape could be committed on a female child under ten years old." The clause clarified that it could.[53] Here again, however, a clause ostensibly intended to clarify has caused further confusion.

The 1575–6 Act and the Age of Consent

In the *Second Part of the Institutes*, Coke specifically aligns the age of consent with the age of consent to marriage, that is, twelve. In *The Third Part of the Institutes*, he defines rape as applying to "any woman above the age of ten years against her will, or of a woman child under the age of ten years with her will, or against her will."[54] He interprets the 1575–6 clause, not as clarifying an anomaly, but as superseding the centuries-old accepted age of twelve. Hale summarises Coke's position: "if were she above the age of ten years, and with her will, it should not be rape." However, he points

[50] Ibid., *Statutes*, IV, part I, 617.

[51] Ibid., 618.

[52] Coke, *The Third Part*, 60; T.E., *The Lawes Resolutions*, 401; Dyer, *Reports of cases*, III, sig 3Y3, although it should be noted that Dyer does not necessarily make a causal link between the rape of the child and the clause: he simply adds a footnote to his report acknowledging that by Elizabeth's statute such a case is now within the scope of the law.

[53] Hale, *Historia Placitorum Coronae*, I, 630 (numbered 730).

[54] Coke, *Second Part*, 181; Ibid., The *Third Part*, chapter 11, 60 (sig. F5^r). (In the *Second Part*, in the same paragraph, he affirms the age of consent as twelve Coke alludes to his chapter on rape in *The Third Part* in which he states it to be ten.)

out that the clause only takes on that meaning because "My lord Coke adds the words, *either with her will or against her will*...but the statute gives no such intimation, only declares that such carnal knowledge is rape."[55] Coke's interpretation created the perverse situation that a girl of ten or eleven years might consent to sex *outside* marriage, but not to sex *within* marriage until she was twelve. Yet it was still apparently followed by courts throughout the eighteenth century. Anthony Simpson finds that Coke's interpretation whereby the 1575–6 clause only protected girls under ten effectively introduced a new offence: "unlawful and carnal knowledge of children" (under ten), while creating doubt about girls between ten and twelve years.[56] Even under Hale's interpretation, doubt that a child of such a young age could be an effective witness limited the prospect for appeals of felony under Westminster II.[57] Garthine Walker also cites Simpson, when she rightly points out that rather than resolving an anomaly, the 1575–6 statute "created an ambiguity" in relation to the age of consent and rape victims.[58] Certainly, it is not clear what was the intention of the relevant clause, and we know that two eminent justices at different times disagreed on its interpretation. We also know that there is an absence of relevant case law recorded in the decades of the late-sixteenth to early-seventeenth centuries. It is, therefore, important that discussion about the age of consent takes account of these issues.

Characterised by lack of clarity and ambiguity, the law had evolved from Westminster I and II so that, theoretically, rape or elopement was a capital offence. But while appeals could be brought by fathers, brothers or responsible male relatives, under Westminster II a woman who was raped, and did not consent before or afterwards, retained a right to appeal that

[55] Hale, *Historia Placitorum Coronae*, I, 630 (incorrectly numbered 730). On the age of consent, see also 631(incorrectly numbered 731).

[56] Simpson, "Vulnerability," 184–184 (184). The age of consent to marriage remained twelve years until the last quarter of the nineteenth century (Ibid., 185). See also Edelstein, "Rape and Malicious Prosecution," 352, note 6).

[57] Hale, *Historia Placitorum Coronae*, I, 634–35.

[58] Garthine Walker, *Crime, Gender*, 56, note 164. Simpson, "Vulnerability," finds that, in the period 1730–1830, courts throughout the country still accepted Coke's position "without reservation" (187). Although he acknowledges that acceptance by eighteenth-century courts of Coke's interpretation "had an unsound basis in statute and in common law," he nonetheless finds the "revision...implicit in the 1576 Act" (186). If Coke's view had become well established by that time, it probably had within his own—well before Hale's legal career began. (And although the manuscript was in circulation for decades beforehand, Hale's *Historia Placitorum Coronae* was not published until 1736.)

pre-dated the statute. Although, in terms of the statutes, the origins are unclear, the right can be traced to the statute of Merton and The Office of the Coroner.[59]

The Abduction Acts

Enduring confusion about the terms 'rape' and 'ravishment' are bound up with the question of defining rape as a physical violation or as a property crime. In Chap. 2, it was noted that the words "defoulled," "deflower," "violating" and "defiled" are used in the abduction statutes to describe the offence against a woman in what was primarily a crime against property. The words 'rape' and 'ravish' are not. Although Kelly argues that all the statutes comprise one sequence, he acknowledges that, in those identified here as specifically concerned with abduction, "the ambiguous word 'ravish' is avoided." Not only is he noting its absence, but its ambiguity when present.[60] Bearing in mind that usage has caused confusion among legal practitioners over centuries, it would seem unwise for the non-specialist to overburden individual words in constructing an argument about how women, or the crime was regarded historically.

The first of the sequence of Abduction Acts makes clear the interests the sequence was devised to protect. Henry VII's 1487 act was drafted exclusively in relation to women "havyng substaunce…and sume beying heires apparaunte." It made a felony of "Taking awaye Women against their Wills" for their "lucre" and forcing them into marriage. It also encompassed all those who aided and abetted the abductors—a point utilised for dramatic effect in the play, *The Maid in the Mill*. After Florimell's abduction, her father, Franio, the Miller, notes that the law will "hang'em all who had a hand in it." And once Florimell is rescued, King Philippo's question, "Maid, were you stolne?" seeks to determine whether abduction or elopement caused her disappearance.[61] However, in reality, since abduction involving sexual violation was already a felony and a capital offence, even if the victim consented after, there seems little need for the

[59] Coke, *Second Part*, 433.

[60] The terms used are as follows: "defoulled," in *Statutes of the Realm*, II (1816), 512, 3 Henry VII, c. ii, 1487, "deflower" and "violating" in Ibid., IV, part I, 329 (1819), 4 and 5 Philip and Mary, c. viii, 1557–8, and "defiled" in Ibid., IV, part II (1819), 910, 39 Elizabeth I, c. ix, 1597; Kelly, "Statutes of Rapes," 376–77 (376).

[61] *Statutes*, II, (1816), 512, 3 Henry VII, c. ii, 1487; Fletcher and Rowley, *Maid in the Mill*, ed. Bowers, III. 1. 55, V. 2. 160.

introduction of a new act. Ives refers to the "comprehensive code" provided by existing legislation and notes the act was, in its greater part, a restatement of existing law. He therefore considers it "a curiosity – in the main superfluous and for the rest impermanent." It is an assessment consistent with his doubts about Henry VII's reputation as a law-maker, and suggests that other priorities than good governance lay behind the legislation.[62]

The 1487 act added only two details to the existing rape law as it applied to abduction. One was that accessories were now treated as principals (they could be tried without waiting for the main offender to be convicted). The other was more significant, but depended on apparent inconsistency in the wording of the act. The preamble of the act refers to women having "been oft tymes taken by mysdoers cont'rie to their Will, and after maried to such mysdoers or to other by their assent, or defoulled." However, the enacting clause refers only to the taking of "eny Woman soo ayenst her Will." It does not demand a forced marriage or rape (crimes already punishable under the law)—only an abduction. Ives confirms that "a handful of indictments" show the act to have been used in this way. The cases most likely to fall within its authority were those of kidnapping of a minor. Ives finds four cases between 1488 and 1497 of which two victims were specified as children, and in three the kidnappers were labourers—one group known to be from the underworld.[63]

It is doubtful though that the abduction of wealthy women was particularly prevalent. Of fifty-three rape cases in the ten years prior to the act, Ives finds only one which might qualify under the preamble; and although abduction had been a problem in earlier times, there are no recorded cases after 1466. Eventually, the privileging of the enacting clause over the preamble was acknowledged to be a distortion of the act, and a judgment of 1556–7 ruled that felony required the abduction to have been aggravated by rape or forced marriage—a ruling which required further legislation.[64] The first abduction act therefore appears to be an unnecessary intervention in an already complex area of law with established and punitive remedies.

The 1487 act is, in fact, a further example of the crown's response to a single event. Ives recounts a king's bench indictment of the abduction, in

[62] Ives, "Agaynst taking awaye," 24, 25.

[63] Ibid., 25.

[64] The second abduction act: see below.

1487, of the widowed Margery Ruyton from her father John Beaufitz's house by Robert Bellingham and various accomplices. Beaufitz was landed, wealthy and held various public and crown offices. Margery had inherited from her late husband, and was heir to the remaining Beaufitz fortune. Bellingham's precise status was unknown, although he and a main accomplice, Thomas Wodeshawe, held positions in the king's household. The crown's reaction was violent and unprecedented. The chief justice, with other leading judiciary and members of the king's council, assembled on the direct instructions of Henry VII to oversee the issue of indictments against the abductors. Although the five principals surrendered, the prosecution collapsed: no evidence was forthcoming and the crown was left with no case. The likely explanation is collusion between the parties—presumably in their mutual interests. Ives tells us that Bellingham "certainly married his victim and when Beaufitz drew up his will in 1488, he left Bellingham his best silver cup." The most significant aspect of the case would seem to be Henry's reaction. The indictment hints that the primary concern was the apparent challenge to the king's authority by members of his own household and its wider implications: two other statutes passed in the same year concerned "field assembly rout" and "a special procedure to investigate suspected conspiracy in the king's entourage." The real issue had been "the identity of [Margery Ruyton's] abductors" rather than abduction itself.[65]

Ives analyses the workings of the act through the only sufficiently documented case. Margaret Kebell, like Margery Ruyton, was a widow, wealthy through both marriage and her own prospective inheritance, and also abducted by a member of another well-connected family. The incident was perpetrated in 1502 by Roger Vernon of Wirksworth, the son and heir of Sir Henry Vernon of Haddon. The 1487 abduction act proved "useless against the influential," and the king again instigated swift action. In this case though, Henry brought about a negotiated settlement by prerogative, and the Vernons were pardoned on payment of various "considerations."[66] But neither statute nor common law had been effective, and the outcome relied in part on Margaret's determined persistence, and part on the king's executive power.

The act, 4 & 5 Philip and Mary, c. 8 (1557–8) was the result of a 1556–7 ruling that to become a felony, abduction must be aggravated by

[65] Ives, "Agaynst taking awaye," 26–30 (28, 29).

[66] Ibid., 41, 42. See 31–44 for a detailed account of the case.

rape or forced marriage.[67] If the 1487 act was "a curiosity" and "superfluous," it seems the second abduction act is equally anomalous. The heading of the 1557–8 act refers specifically to "the Punishment of suche as shall take awaye Maydens that bee Inheritoures, being within thage of xvi yeres, or that marrie them without Consent of their Parentes." The preamble then describes the daughters of "Noblemen Gentlemen and others, aswell suche as be Heires Apparente" and their inheritance of various forms; two references simply to "Children," follow. B.J. and Mary Sokol apparently take the wording to indicate the inclusion of male as well as female heirs when they say that the statute "addressed those who stole heirs and heiresses"—but they do not elaborate.[68] However, the first enacting clause and all subsequent clauses specify the victim as "Mayde" or "Woman Childe." The same is true throughout the marginal headings: the preamble is summarised stating the act's object as: "Evil of Abduction and marriage of *Heiresses*, &c. without Consent of their Parents &c" [my emphasis]. Crucially, all five of the relevant enacting clauses specify female children.[69]

The act was aimed at "persons of lewde demeanour" and "unthriftie and light personages" who use "flattery trifling Giftes and faire promises" to lure their victims:

> Either with slight or force oftentymes [to] be taken and conveied away from their said Parentes Freends or Kynnsfolkes, to the highe displeasure of Almightie God, disparagement of the said Children and thextreme contynuall heviness of all their Freendes.

The purpose of the offenders was described as to "bye and sell the said Maidens and Children," in order "to contracte Matrimonie." Victims were assumed to be unwilling, or gullible—even if complicit.

However, despite clarifying the difference between abduction with and without sexual violation, the 1557–8 act seems substantially to have downgraded both crimes from capital felony. The second enacting clause made the penalty for abduction two years' imprisonment, or a fine in Star

[67] *Statutes*, IV, part I, 329, 4 and 5 Philip and Mary, c. viii, 1557–8.

[68] Sokol, *Shakespeare, Law, and Marriage*, 109.

[69] See also the preamble to the 1487 act, and to the final abduction statute, discussed below: 39 Elizabeth I, chapter 9. Both include in their respective preambles various categories of women, referring specifically to the status of some as heirs apparent, but both acts are unequivocally for the protection of females only.

Chamber. If the offender should "deflower any such Mayde or Woman Childe," or "contracte Matrimonie" against the will of the father (mother or guardian), the third clause states the penalty will be five years or a fine. Notably, this is the first of either sequence of statutes to use the term "children" in referring to those about whom so much of the legislation is concerned. The words "Woman Childe" would later specify those under ten years who were protected by the final, 1575–6, rape statute, otherwise the usual categories of "women," "maids," "maidens" and "damsels" ignore the youth of those often involved in incidents of rape and abduction. In this case, the word "children" draws attention to the characteristics of innocence and naiveté the act aims to emphasise in the process of legislating for those under sixteen years.

Yet one effect of the act is to add to the confused thinking around age. The second clause specifies that the penalty applies to offenders from the age of fourteen. Since the age of consent for girls is twelve, it raises a further anomaly about perceptions of age, gender and behaviour. Hale puzzles that "an infant under the age of fourteen years is presumed by law unable to commit a rape, and therefore it seems cannot be guilty of it…as to this fact the law presumes him impotent, as well as wanting discretion." It is an irony, indeed when a girl child of ten can be held responsible for her sexual integrity.[70]

Under the fourth clause of the 1557–8 act, "Starre Chamber…shall have authorite by virtue of this Act to here and determyne the sayd Offences," while "suche Processe shall bee awarded and lye, as upon an Indictmente of Trespas at the Common Lawe." Abduction of an heiress under age sixteen, with or without violation or forced marriage, had become a common law trespass with limited penalties. And in attempting to clarify one matter, the 1557–8 act produced three anomalies. First, it apparently contradicts the rape statutes which already defined abduction with sexual violation as rape. (At this stage in their evolution, rape and elopement were capital felonies, with only one recourse to clergy, and no protection of sanctuary.) Second, if a case for violation is brought under its provisions rather than under rape law, it actually weakens the pre-existing deterrent of felony. Third, if Philip and Mary's act for those under sixteen years was intended to run alongside Henry VII's act, this would still leave an anomaly in respect of acts of non-violation against those over sixteen.

[70] *Statutes*, IV, part I, 329, 4 and 5 Philip and Mary, c. viii, 1557–8; Hale, *Historia Placitorum Coronae*, I, 630 (incorrectly numbered 730).

It is unclear why the crime which had attracted such anxiety among those determined to protect their opportunities for accumulation of wealth and estates should be diminished by written law in this way. It might simply represent the actuality that common law trespass proved a more successful suit than felony.

Finally, in the abduction sequence, Elizabeth I introduces "An Acte for the taking away of Cleargy from Offendors against a certaine Statute made in the Thirde yeare of the Raigne of King Henry the Seaventh, concerning the taking away of Weomen against their Wills unlawfully."[71] Significantly, the preamble refers directly back to 3 Henry VII, chapter 2, with no mention of the 1557–8 act, confirming that the statute of 1487 had not been superseded. This final act refers to the offence as a felony, and similarly to the two previous abduction acts, it includes "divers Weomen, as well Maydens as Widdowes and Wyves, having Substance…and some being Heires Apparent." There is, again, no suggestion that any age-group is either specifically included or excluded, and it can be read to include all females. It is not clear where this leaves the 1557–8 act, but effectively 39 Elizabeth I, chapter 9 (1597) brings abduction back in line with rape law and other felonies for which there was capital punishment without clergy.

In practice, the 1597 act marks a return to the pre-1487 situation when an act of sexual violation per se, elopement or abduction each attracted the same penalty. In doing so, however, it provided no greater clarity than before: the range of legislation under which appeals could be brought meant that the opportunities for legal manoeuvring, obscurity and confusion were proportionately enhanced—whether for those embroiled in the system at the time, or for those engaging with it historically.

Women, Wards and Wardship

In the late Tudor period, both Henry VII and Henry VIII relied on the exploitation of the king's feudal authority to increase their power and wealth. The crown and the aristocracy alike benefited from developing alliances with members of the court, which also eased the demands for both a bureaucracy and an army. It was a role in which aristocratic women appear to have been particularly effective. Hundreds of letters by women survive concerning "grants of land, annuities, Crown offices, wardships, and places at court; assistance defending their inheritances and dowers or

[71] *Statutes*, IV, part II, 910, 39 Elizabeth I, c. ix, 1597.

jointures; protection against brutal or neglectful spouses; and exemption from the penalties of forfeiture imposed on their husbands."[72] In addition to furthering family interests, the evidence shows that women looked to the king's prerogative to redress the inequity they faced in marital disputes, or where their own financial status was threatened, or, as in the case of Margaret Kebell, where the law proved ineffective.

The practice of wardship dated back beyond the mid-thirteenth century and continued until its abolition in 1646. It was, therefore, as we have seen, an important consideration throughout the progress of the rape statutes, bearing in mind that Kelly argues that the rape statutes refer back to the 1235 Statute of Merton concerned the loss of a ward's marriage value. Chapter 35 of Westminster II concerns ravishment of wards: "Children Males or Females, whose Marriage belongeth to another, taken and carried away."[73] Carrying away a ward was not a felony, but it carried a two-year penalty if the ward was restored, and exile or life imprisonment if not. The detailed and lengthy chapter reemphasises the priority given to inheritance rights.

If a tenant-in-chief of the crown died leaving a daughter under age fourteen as his heiress, the king gained the girl's wardship. This gave him custody of her body and, in such cases, "the right to arrange [her] marriages and collect the profits from [her] estates."[74] The same rule applied to males up to the age of twenty-one. Theoretical safeguards protecting young men from abuse of the system were sufficiently costly to deter heirs from taking legal suit against their guardians. There was a highly competitive market within the court to buy wardships from the king, and these might be sold-on time and again for profit, or to gain advantage from disposal of the marriage.[75] By Tudor times, the trade in wardships was prevalent amongst the ruling classes and gentry when women played a significant part. Henry VIII's papers show that women were active participants in the trade.[76]

[72] Harris, "View," 222–23 (223), tells us that the letters can be found "in Henry VIII's State Papers, the Cotton Manuscripts, in the British Library, and other public and private archival collections."

[73] *Statutes*, I, 87, 13 Edward I, c. xxxiv–xxxv, 1285.

[74] Harris, "View," 227. Brewer, *By Birth of Consent*, 292–296. But see also Hurstfield, "Lord Burghley," 96. Hurstfield gives the age below which girls were liable to wardship as 16.

[75] Hurstfield, "Lord Burghley," 95–96.

[76] Harris, "View," 223, and 241, referring particularly to the activities of Lady Margaret Beaufort in the marriage market—although patronage and/or friendship rather than wardship might describe her interest.

Amidst the objectified status statutory rape law imposed on women, particularly those from families of substance, the various ways in which women negotiated their position within those limitations should not be overlooked. Despite the law closing off means by which they might assert their own choice in marriage, women also exploited the system using their capabilities to form alliances and to gain influence and advantage for their families and themselves.

"History cannot be written from the statute books alone"

For non-specialist critics, Nazife Bashar's influential claims that "rape was separated from abduction in statutes of 1555 and 1597" (see Chap. 1) has added to the confusion and error compounded as critics attempt further to develop the theme in relation to social history.[77] It is particularly unfortunate when the material is used, not just as context, but as the basis for an overall argument. The following examples are representative of many such. They vary in significance, but have variously attracted extensive citation in their turn. Their role here is to demonstrate how misinformation spreads exponentially and the implication of potential misreading for individual works. In two examples from Shakespeare criticism, Barbara Bowen and Emily Detmer-Goebel fall prey to the problem of rape and abduction. The relationship between property and rape is central to Bowen's argument when she discusses the 1487 act as a continuation of rape law. Her error is compounded by a misquotation from the statute in which she finds that women are described as "'like Goods, oftentimes taken by Misdoers'." The phrase "like goods" does not describe victims in the 1487 act, nor in either of the other two similarly-worded abduction acts of 1557 and 1597.[78] Detmer-Goebel is led to base a significant strand of her argument on Bashar's misinterpretation of the statutes in her paper, "The Need for Lavinia's Voice." She notes "the culture's ambiguous attitude towards a woman's revelation of rape" and makes a number of erroneous

[77] The section heading is from Sue Sheridan Walker, "Punishing Convicted Ravishers", 237.

[78] Bashar, "Rape in England", 41; Bowen, "Aemilia Lanyer's *Lucrece*", 116. *Statutes*, II, 512, 3 Henry VII, c. ii, 1487, reads: "Where wymmen as well [Maydens] as Wydowes and Wyfes having substaunce some in goods moveable, and some in landes and tenants, and sume beyng heires apparaunt unto their auncestors, for the lucre of suche substaunce been oft tymes taken by mysdoers…"

or misguided proposals based both on Bashar's misreading and unproductive attempts at semantic distinctions between 'rape' and 'ravishment'. She suggests that the dramatic tension created in early modern drama "might be due, in part, to relatively recent changes in the law of rape." In her discussion of *Titus*, she calls Saturninus's reference to abduction as rape, "an increasingly rare usage." In the correct context this might be so, bearing in mind that after 1487, abduction is not referred to as rape within the abduction acts. However, in *Titus*, there is a strong implication that Lavinia is willing and complicit with Bassanius, so that there is a question of elopement (rape) rather than abduction. The abduction acts of 1487 and 1597 insist on the words "against their will," while elopement remained vulnerable to rape law.[79]

Both Catherine Belsey and Laurie Maguire assert a link between the incorrect interpretation of the statutes and the question of consent. Situating the appearance of Shakespeare's *Lucrece* at a time when rape "was changing its meaning," Belsey claims that in 1594 rape "included abduction." After reprising Bashar's misleading assumption in relation to the Elizabethan statutes, she adds a dependent clause, erroneously asserting that "for the first time the legal issue began to be seen, however tentatively, as one of consent."[80] However, the word is significant to rape law from the earliest times. As discussed in Chap. 2, it is at the heart of the doctrine that consent is necessary to conception—a dogma that originated in the Greek philosophy of Hippocrates, to be transmitted over the centuries via Galenic theory and Christian theology into medieval England, and early modern common law.[81]

Although, in her 2009 monograph about Helen of Troy, Maguire displaces a central fallacy of her 2006 paper that "[r]ape was a term which was being redefined in the 1590s," she reiterates the various misunderstandings that vex the earlier work. In a section devoted to the 1597 abduction act, the discussion follows Bashar's misleading assertion about the separation of rape and abduction. As a corollary, Maguire attributes the statute with the origins of the legal significance of consent in appeals of rape—an assertion that this final abduction act somehow introduced both the concept and the word 'consent' into rape law. As we have seen, consent was significant throughout the statutes in any distinction between

[79] Detmer-Goebel, "Lavinia's Voice," 77–79 (78), 91, note 18.

[80] Belsey, "Tarquin Dispossessed," 333, 316, 333.

[81] The discussion in Chap. 2 is based on Histed, "Mediaeval Rape," 743–69.

rape, elopement and abduction.[82] It must be remembered though, that reiteration of Bashar's claims for changes in rape law at the end of the sixteenth century has become commonplace in criticism.

Poor drafting, lack of clarity, anomaly and contradiction characterise the rape and abduction statutes. The fact that there were four instances when a single event possibly caused the crown to amend or introduce legislation demonstrates the importance of balancing historical context with assumptions about public attitudes to the crimes. It is apparent that lack of context and incomplete reading can lead to overdetermination or misunderstanding of the law's meaning or intentions in its particular historical time, and in ours debate continues among the legal professionals. For the non-specialist critic, the consequent difficulty of interpretation contributes to the temptation to overdetermine the individual meaning of the statutes. Misunderstandings about the status of various treatises and handbooks, and unjustified weight given to imprecise terminology and common law practice described in Chap. 2, results in confusion that is difficult to unpick. A particular difficulty in clarifying misunderstandings in modern criticism is the compound misinterpretations that accumulate when several sources and misreadings are combined. It is only by reference to the statutes in sequence and with an awareness of their context, ambiguity and limitations that early modern rape law can be discussed coherently.

The statutes define rape not merely in semantic terms, nor those of the direct personal meaning to the victim, but in terms by which it had meaning in that society: social order, the making and consolidating of family fortunes, the crown coffers, the sovereign's authority, the relationship between individuals and the state and its status as one among other felonies. If it is tempting for us to make judgments about the material focus of the law from a position in the present, we should not forget the nature of the times. However distasteful we might now find the play, in Shakespeare's *The Taming of the Shrew*, Katherina reminds us of a man's lot: he "commits his body | To painful labour both by sea and land, | To watch the night in storms, the day in cold."[83] The words are a reminder of the quotidian brutality prevalent during the period in history under consideration: men were obliged to go to war and fight hand to hand with crude and

[82] Maguire, "Helen of Troy," 31; Ibid., *From Homer to Hollywood*, 101–102.
[83] Shakespeare, *Taming of the Shrew*, ed. Ann Thompson, V. 2, 148–50.

vicious weapons, while courts handed down often cruel physical punishments for criminal and social transgressions.

Over the three-hundred-year period during which statutory rape law developed, the priorities and culture were also evolving. We cannot assume the proportions in which any abhorrence expressed in the written law of rape can be distributed between its various meanings at any particular historical moment: loss of wealth, loss of honour, disparagement of the actions of the offender, sympathy for the injury of, or disgust at, the now despoiled victim. And it might be perverse from a modern point of view, on the one hand, to condemn the secondary status allocated to women while, on the other, expressing dismay that rape was not more frequently redressed by mutilations and hangings.

Bibliography

Baker, John. *The Oxford History of the Laws of England*, vol. 6, edited by John Baker. Oxford: Oxford University Press, 2003- (2003).

Bashar, Nazife. "Rape in England between 1550 and 1700", in *The Sexual Dynamics of History: Men's Power, Women's Resistance*. The London Feminist History Group. London: Pluto, 1983.

Belsey, Catherine. "Tarquin Dispossessed: Expropriation and Consent in *The Rape of Lucrece*", *Shakespeare Quarterly*, 52 (2001): 315–55.

Bowen, Barbara. "The Rape of Jesus: Aemilia Lanyer's *Lucrece*", in *Marxist Shakespeares*, edited by Jean E. Howard, and Scott Cutler Shershow. London: Routledge, 2001.

Brewer, Holly. *By Birth or Consent: Children, Law, and the Anglo-American Revolution in Authority*. Chapel Hill: University of North Carolina Press, 2007.

Bracton, Henricus de. *De Legibus et Consuetudinibus Angliae. Bracton*, edited by George E. Woodbine, translated by Samuel E. Thorne. Vol 2. Cambridge, Mass.: Harvard University Press, 1968.

Chaytor, Miranda. "Husband(ry): Narratives of Rape in the Seventeenth Century", *Gender and History*, 7 (1995): 378–407.

Coke, Edward. *Institutes of the Laws of England*, 4 vols. New York and London: Garland, 1979.

———. *The Second Part of the Institutes of the Lawes of England*. London: Brooke, 1797.

———. *The Third Part of the Institutes of the Laws of England*, 4th edition. London: Brooke, 1797.

Dalton, Michael. *The countrey justice containing the practice of the justices of the peace out of their sessions*. London: Islip, 1618; 1619; 1622; 1626.

Davenport, Robert (?). *Dick of Devonshire*, edited by G. James, and Mary R. McManaway, The Malone Society, Vol. 103. British Museum Ms Egerton 1994, folios 30–51; repr. 1955.

Detmer-Goebel, Emily. "The Need for Lavinia's Voice: *Titus Andronicus* and the Telling of Rape", *Shakespeare Studies*, 29 (2001): 75–92.

Dunn, Caroline. *Stolen Women in Medieval England: Rape, Abduction and Adultery*. Cambridge: Cambridge University Press, 2013.

Dyer, James. *Reports of cases in the reigns of Hen. VIII, Edw. VI, Q. Mary, And Q. Eliz, Taken and collected by Sir James Dyer, Knt, Some time Chief Justice*. Vol 3. London: sold by Butterworth, 1794.

Edelstein, Laurie. "An Accusation Easily to be Made: Rape and Malicious Prosecution in Eighteenth Century England", *The American Journal of Legal History*, 42 (1998): 351–90.

E[dgar] T[homas]. *The Lawes Resolutions of Womens Rights: Or, The Lawes Provision for Woemen*. London: More, 1632.

Fletcher, John, and William Rowley. The Maid in the Mill, edited by Fredson Bowers, in Vol 9 of *The Dramatic Works in the Beaumont and Fletcher Canon*, edited by Bowers. Cambridge: Cambridge University Press,1994.

Hale, Matthew. *Historia Placitorum Coronae* 2 vols. 1736. Reprint, London: Professional Books, 1971.

———. *The History of the Common Law in England*, edited by Charles M. Gray. 1713. Reprint, 1739. Reprint, London: University of Chicago Press, 1971.

Harris, Barbara J. "The View from My Lady's Chamber: New Perspectives on the Early Tudor Monarchy", *Huntington Library Quarterly*, 60 (1997): 215–47.

Histed, Elise Bennett. "Mediaeval Rape: A Conceivable Defence?", *Cambridge Law Journal*, 63 (2004): 743–69.

Hurstfield, J. "Lord Burghley as Master of the Court of Wards, 1561–98", *Transactions of the Royal Historical Society*, 4th series, 31 (1949): 95–114.

Ives, E. W. "'Agaynst taking awaye of Women': The Inception and Operation of the Abduction Act of 1487", in *Wealth and Power in Tudor England: Essays Presented to S.T. Bindoff*, edited by E. W. Ives, R.J. Knecht and J.J. Scarisbrick. London: Athlone Press, 1978.

Kelly, Henry Ansgar. "Statutes of Rapes and Alleged Ravishers of Wives: A Context for the Charges against Thomas Mallory, Knight", *Viator: Medieval and Renaissance Studies* 28. (1997): 361–419.

Kesselring, K.J. "Felony Forfeiture and the Profits of Crime in Early Modern England", *The Historical Journal*, 53.2 (2010): 271–88.

Maguire, Laurie. *Helen of Troy: From Homer to Hollywood*. Chichester: Wiley-Blackwell, 2009.

———. "Helen of Troy: Representing Absolute Beauty in Language", *Sederi*, 16 (2006): 31–51.

Post, J. B. "Ravishment of Women and the Statutes of Westminster", in *Legal Records and the Historian: Papers Presented to the Cambridge Legal History Conference, 7–10 July 1975*, edited by J. H. Baker. London: Royal Historical Society, 1978.

———. "Sir Thomas West and the Statute of Rapes, 1382", *Bulletin of Historical Research*, 53 (1980): 24–30

Shakespeare, William. *The Taming of the Shrew*, edited by Ann Thompson. 1984. Reprint, The New Cambridge Shakespeare. Cambridge: Cambridge University Press, 2001.

Sharpe, J. A. *Crime in Early Modern England 1550–1750*, 2nd edition. London: Longman, 1999

Simpson, Antony E. "Vulnerability and the Age of Female Consent: Legal Innovation and Its Effect on Prosecutions for Rape in Eighteenth-Century London", in *Sexual Worlds of the Enlightenment*, edited by G. S. Rousseau and Roy Porter. Manchester: Manchester University Press, 1987.

Sokol, B. J., and Mary. *Shakespeare, Law, and Marriage*. Cambridge: Cambridge University Press, 2003.

Statutes of the Realm, 12 vols. London: England Record Commission, 1810–1828.

Toner, Barbara. *The Facts of Rape*. London: Arrow, 1977.

Walker, Garthine. *Crime, Gender and Social Order in Early Modern England*. Cambridge: Cambridge University Press, 2003.

Walker, Sue Sheridan. "Punishing Convicted Ravishers: Statutory Strictures and Actual Practice in Thirteenth and Fourteenth-Century England", *Journal of Medieval History* 13 (1987): 237–50.

CHAPTER 4

The Lawes Resolutions of Womens Rights

Abstract Given the ostensibly succinct summary of rape statutes set out in *The Lawes Resolutions*, and the author's commentary on the origins of law, it is unsurprising that critics have regarded it as a useful source for legal context. However, the treatise was without legal authority in its own time and its guidance on rape should be treated with caution in ours. This chapter reviews the history of its production and its representation of rape law. Importantly for those exploring the treatise today, it identifies where critical misreadings arise in relation to rape law, and the impact on criticism that might, in its turn, mislead. Errors in the treatise's representation of statute law, and a sometimes mischievous tone, are warnings of its equivocal status. Coupled with questions about its authorship, potential readership, and the circumstances surrounding its production, these elements suggest that the treatise was a speculative project aimed at exploiting the emerging print trade—of which law books were a profitable part. To avoid further compounding existing errors, and to alert the reader to the potential unreliability of *The Lawes Resolutions*, the chapter identifies problematic interpretations that have gained critical currency.

Keywords The Lawes Resolutions • Rape law • Law books and the print trade

H. Barker, *Rape in Early Modern England*,
https://doi.org/10.1007/978-3-030-82609-3_4

The apparent historical incongruity of the concern for the 'rights' of women expressed in the title of the seventeenth-century *The Lawes Resolutions of Womens Rights: or The Lawes Provision for Woemen* might hint at the uncertain status of the treatise as a legal authority.[1] Yet the fund of information it contains about the legal position of women—extracts from statutes, commentary, and observation—has proved irresistible to those seeking a concise source of information. However, it cannot be relied on as a legal source, but should be viewed with more caution, as a trade book, a product of the burgeoning printing industry.

The Lawes Resolutions also carries the running title *The Womans Lawyer*. It is a legal treatise, printed anonymously in 1632, "which comprehends all our Lawes concerning Women."[2] The work has attracted scholarship of two types: for one—those concerned with the circumstances of its production or analysis of its content—it is an object of historiography, and for the other, it is examined as a legal source document in its own right. A sense of ambiguity about the treatise soon becomes apparent from those engaged with scholarship of the first type. Wilfrid Prest wondered at its "use…by anyone other than lawyers and law students," involving as it does "the examination of abstruse theoretical issues arising from…largely obsolete statute law." Yet, despite its "unpromising subject matter and adoption of at least some of the conventions of orthodox legal literature," he nonetheless finds it "a surprisingly lively, even entertaining book." On the other hand, Doris Stenton finds it "stiff reading," while admiring the ability and education of those women who might have coped with it (if, indeed, they did). Peter Goodrich sees its theme as "the defence of women"; at the same time, some of its advice at least is "in part ironic." Mary Polito describes it as "produced by legal practitioners for a lay reading public"; by providing "an extremely thorough summary" of the major legal sources, it enables women to "protect themselves and their estates from duplicitous, land hungry men." And its perceived stance of offering help to those who were legally disadvantaged by their status as women was, according to Christopher Cannon, "provocative."[3]

[1] T.E., *Lawes Resolutions*.

[2] *Lawes Resolutions*, "The Epistle to the Reader," sig. a1^{v}.

[3] Prest, "Law and Women's Rights," 177, 181; Stenton, *The English Woman*, 61; Goodrich, "Gynaetopia: Feminine Genealogies," 292; Polito, "Wit, Will and Governance," 16, and 24; Christopher Cannon, "Rights," 160.

Although there is some consensus that the treatise is thorough in its scope (if not in detail), critics from all fields of interest struggle to find a coherent voice within it. Those using *The Lawes Resolutions* as a legal source are inclined to ignore, or forgive its sometimes mischievous tone. They inevitably find themselves mediating between its ostensible support for women, and the frequently witty and ironic terms in which it is offered. Whichever voice the reader chooses to hear, the text requires careful scrutiny alongside commentary and analysis by recognised legal sources.

There is much speculation and little certainty about the origins and purpose of *The Lawes Resolutions*, compounded by the question of its authorship. But some anomalies are diminished if, in addition to its apparent ideology or authorial intention, its publication is considered from the viewpoint of commercial opportunism. In this wider context, a range of factors collude to suggest how and when it came to be published. These factors can be identified in the background of those involved with the production of the treatise, in the histories of the early modern print trade and of legal education and publishing, and in the structures of and access to the law. And so, although the treatise remains a useful reference point if addressed within a more widely informed exploration of early modern law concerning women, unless the circumstances surrounding its production are taken into account, it can mislead the unwary.

Authorship

The BL catalogue shows two imprints of *The Lawes Resolutions*, both dated 1632. One is "printed by [Miles Flesher for] the assignes of John More Esq.," the other "by the assignment of John More Esquire." It was never re-printed. The book was entered in the Stationers' register "under the handes of" Sir Egremont Thynne and Thomas Edgar on 30 April 1632, and was to be sold by John Grove.[4] In 1618, John More, by whose assigns *The Lawes Resolutions* was printed, was granted the patent to print law books for forty years from 1628 or 1629. He assigned those rights to Miles Flesher and his partners John Haviland and Robert Young on 1 May 1629 in return for an agreement to pay £60 a year plus one third of the profits. There is no record of him ever having printed in his own right.[5]

[4] *ESTC* Citation no. S100217, System no. 006171899; STC Citation (2nd edn), 7437.

[5] Plomer, *Dictionary of the Booksellers*, 76, s.v. Fletcher, or Flesher (Miles), 131, s.v. More, John.

The Preface to *The Lawes Resolutions* is signed "I.L." (or "J.L.") in which the writer states that the work was "long since collected," and the author "dead."[6] The Epistle to the Reader is signed "T. E.," one who also describes having amended and revised the work "having a Copie thereof lying by me…within …a Lent vacation." This description of T. E.'s involvement, together with Thomas Edgar's name in the Stationers' register, has led to the (probably reasonable) assumption that these are both the same man, and of his association with authorship of the treatise.[7]

T. E. certainly claims editorship, but if his claim is true, speculation must still surround the origins of the manuscript to which he applied his editorial attention—whether it was indeed the work of an earlier, deceased lawyer, or his own. The *ESTC* notes that the work is "[s]ometimes attributed to Sir John Dodderidge," an eminent late sixteenth- and early seventeenth-century lawyer and judge. Dodderidge died in 1628, some four years before its publication, and this timing might fit with the notion of a work updated with the addition of more recent cases and commentary. However, there is no evidence to substantiate what is a speculative link.[8]

Wilfred Prest has produced probably the most thorough scholarship on *The Lawes Resolutions*, and regards not only its "authorship" but also its "contents and intended audience" as "somewhat mysterious." He begins his enquiry with the question of authorship and, following the BL catalogue's association of T. E. with the name Thomas Edgar, provides a compelling account of a lawyer of that name whose circumstances appear to match those of the putative author too closely for mere coincidence. A "Thomas Edgar was admitted to membership of Gray's Inn in 1619" and called to the bar in 1625. He was born in 1602, and probably attended grammar school in Ipswich, before Cambridge University. He appears to have been a "moderately prosperous" provincial lawyer, who served on the Gray's Inn society's governing body from 1650. Whether significant, ironic or an apposite corollary to his association with *The Lawes Resolutions*, his marriage seems to have been successful: in 1635 he married Mary Poule (or Powell) "the nineteen year old heiress of a London citizen and

[6] *Lawes Resolutions*, Preface, sig. A4r, sig. A3v.

[7] Ibid., sig. a2r. See also Halkett and Laing, *Anonymous and Pseudonymous Publications*, 254, s.v. T.E.

[8] *ESTC*, Citation number S 100217; *Oxford Dictionary of National Biography*, s.v. "Dodderidge [Doddridge] Sir John (1555–1628), judge" (by David Ibbetson). https://doi.org/10.1093/ref:odnb/7745. Accessed 6 April 2021.

merchant tailor, and the grand-daughter of a high-ranking Elizabethan legal bureaucrat." There were ten children of the marriage and when Edgar died aged ninety, he and Mary had been married for fifty-seven years.[9]

Edgar's credentials and career support his candidature for involvement with *The Lawes Resolutions*, as do the apparent dates and citations included in the text.[10] Prest observes that "the original body of the text is not clearly distinguished or distinguishable from Edgar's later additions." However, references to legal reports and notes place the beginning of the original work "no earlier than the mid-1580s," while those to "the late Queen Elizabeth," and the claim to "have…sailed betwixt the capes of *Magna Charta* and Quadragesima of Queen Elizabeth," point to its completion early in James 1's reign.[11] On the other hand, he notes that references to Coke's 1628 publications, *First Institutes*, and the *Commentaries on Littleton*, are likely to represent the work of Edgar. Similarly, "scattered references" to Coke's *Reports* published between 1600 and 1615, and various other citations—for example, unreported cases from 1632—must also be attributable to the later editor.[12]

It is a possibility though, as Prest points out, that Edgar was indeed the author of *The Lawes Resolutions*, and that the late, anonymous author was "a fiction." By 1632, aged only twenty-nine, Edgar's inexperience would have been at odds with the convention of the legal author as "venerable sage." Concern for the book's credibility—and therefore commercial appeal—may well account for the preservation of the author's anonymity.[13] Interestingly though, Prest finds the only other work authored by Edgar was published under his initials, T. E. It, too, is prefaced by a disclaimer explaining that the author's initial opposition was put aside "to prevent mistakes in Copies."[14] The same justification of inexperience to explain the author's coyness cannot be sustained in this case though—a mere thirteen-page political pamphlet published some eighteen years later.

[9] Prest, "Law and Women's Rights," 172–174 (173, 174).

[10] Subsequent references in this text will assume that Prest's Edgar, and T. E. are one and the same, and editor, if not author of the treatise.

[11] Prest, "Law and Women's Rights," 174–75; *Lawes Resolutions*, 196, 389, 400, 403. Polito's claim ("Wit, Will and Governance," 23), that "evidence suggests [the treatise] was written during the latter part of Elizabeth's reign," is misleading.

[12] Prest, "Law and Women's Rights," 175; *Lawes Resolutions*, 187, 225, 276, 322.

[13] Prest, "Law and Women's Rights," 175.

[14] Ibid.; Edgar, *Two Charges*, "Stationer to the Reader," sig. A2^r. The *ESTC* notes that "T. E. = Thomas Edgar."

Finding a Readership

Regardless of its authorship, the contents of *The Lawes Resolutions* have generated persistent interest among those studying early modern culture. Lynne A. Greenberg notes that "quotations from the text are…nearly ubiquitous in recent articles discussing the legal status of the early modern Englishwoman."[15] The law and commentary do provide a remarkably convenient reference for the modern critic. The title page describes the contents: "A Methodicall Collection of such Statutes and Customes, with the Cases, Opinions, Arguments and points of Learning in the Law, as doe properly concerne Women." The treatise contains "the immunities, advantages, interests, and duties of women." The Epistle tells us those women, might be "either Children in government or nurture of their Parents or Guardians, Mayds, Wives, and Widowes," and those concerns include "their goods, inheritances, and other estates." It commends the contents as "profitable and usefull Learning to be well knowne."[16] The treatise is organised to follow the phases of a woman's life and how these are recognised in law—inevitably in terms of the relationship to men. Five "Books" are ordered first to identify the legal implications of the different life-stages, then progress through the contracting of marriage, marriage, widowhood and remarriage. Rape is the subject of the final sections of the last book.

However, despite its accessibility and extensive use today, there is little evidence to support Greenberg's assertion that "legal commentators cited the treatise well into the eighteenth century." The only apparent evidence of its citation as a legal authority is a single example in an early eighteenth-century tract: John Brydall's *Privilegia Magnatum*, where it is offered as one of several sources on a point concerning the remarriage of the widows of noblemen. Greenberg cites Prest as her authority; however, his comment that *The Lawes Resolutions* "continued to be cited into the following century," has possibly been overinterpreted.[17] Two of only three other citations Prest finds are in book catalogues.[18] The third is a mention by William Sheppard, in the preface to *The Touchstone of Common Assurances*,

[15] Greenberg ed., *Legal Treatises*, Part 1, vols 1–3, xxxvi.

[16] *Lawes Resolutions*, title page, 3, and sig. a1^{v}.

[17] Greenberg, *Legal Treatises*, xxxvi, citing cites Prest, "Law and Women's Rights," 187, note 62; John Brydall, *Privilegia magnatum apud Anglos*, 11–12.

[18] The two catalogues cited by Prest are: London, *A Catalogue*, sig. Bb4^{v}, where it is entitled *The Lawes <u>and</u> Resolutions*…[my emphasis], and Worrall, *Bibliotheca legum*, 136.

to justify publication of his own work.[19] In other words, other than one minor example, the treatise is largely disregarded by the legal profession, although it continued on sale and in circulation.

The apparent absence of *The Lawes Resolutions* from citation in serious legal works of the seventeenth century is one of the anomalies surrounding the work, and one of the cautionary signals to be heeded when encountering its presence in modern criticism. There may be several reasons for its lack of professional status, including the subject matter, and the anonymity of the author. Today's critics though, are torn between the convenient access to the law it offers, the cultural insights offered by its commentary, and the apparent ironies and ambiguities with which they are delivered.

When pondering its intentions, an inescapable feature of *The Lawes Resolutions* is the notion of women's rights created by the title, and the risk of allowing an unhistorical modern emphasis to be placed on it. Since any rights accruing to women were so limited, the title is an ironic reminder of the lack of rights enjoyed by those whose legal status was limited by virtue of their sex. It is a point the author expands on early in the text:

> Women…have nothing to do in constituting Lawes, or consenting to them, in interpreting of Lawes, or in hearing them interpreted at lectures, leets or charges, and yet they stand strictly tyed to mens establishments; little or nothing excused by ignorance.[20]

Within the scope of *The Lawes Resolutions*, the word 'rights' sits most comfortably with the predominant preoccupations of early modern England with land and property. Polito perceives this in the author's organisation of the work to follow the changing entitlements to property through the different states and stages of a woman's life.[21] Rape law is a demonstration of how early modern women are always defined by their place within this dynamic. In this context, it is culturally anachronistic to criticise the author of *The Lawes Resolutions*, as Greenberg does, because he "fails to advocate or to encourage legal reform." The stance he actually invokes is for women "to behave virtuously, to live a modest and chast life at home and to look to God and the next life for comfort." But he also does indeed propose women "move for redress" by Parliament for inequi-

[19] Sheppard, *touch-stone of common assurances*, sig. A5^{v}.

[20] *Lawes Resolutions*, 2.

[21] Polito, "Wit, Will and Governance," 26–27.

table land laws between man and wife. He entirely reprises social, political and legal understandings about authority and a woman's place within institutional hierarchies, while also perceiving the law's inequity.[22]

Before moving on from the naming of the work, it is worth noting that the title-page bears the subtitle *The Lawes Provision for Woemen*. The usages of "women" (and its alternatives), "[i]n the 16th and 17th centuries [were] frequently with play on a pseudo-etymological association with *woe*."[23] T. E. later places this usage in the scriptural context of the creation of woman from man, and its signification "not the woe of Man …but with Man …as a helpe, and a companion." Whether its use in the subtitle is facetious or not, the fact of his apparent need to explain, in somewhat convoluted terms of semantics and pronunciation, begs a question of the usage in the first place. Once alerted to the potential irony, it is difficult to ignore that possibility in relation to aspects of the remainder of the text. For example, when the author refers in the Preface to women as "that sexe generally beloved," how firmly might his tongue be in his cheek? And at whom is his irony directed? Is it at "that sexe" or at those entrenched in the ideas espoused within inequitable laws?[24]

Many examples of the author's much-quoted comments and asides throughout the body of the text continue in the apparently humorous vein. In the case of a dower, when a woman only becomes entitled after consummation of the marriage, she is advised: "when supper is done dance a while, leave out the long measures till you be in bed, get you there quickly, and pay the Minstrels tomorrow"—a distinctly arch observation. In another example, Joan Larsen Klein notes the "ironic edge" when the author describes a widow's grief:[25]

> Alas, when she hath lost her husband; her head is cut off, her intellectuall part…gone, the verie faculties of her soule are…all be[numn]ed, di[mm]ed and dazled, so that she cannot thinke or remember when to take rest or refection for her weake body.

However, this assessment of the widow's state is quickly followed by the author's offer of comfort:

[22] Greenberg, *Legal Treatises*, xxxvi; *Lawes Resolutions*, 146.

[23] *OED Online*, s.v. "woman, n": previous version, *OED*, Second Edition, 1989, s.v. "woman, *n*." I. 1. k.

[24] *Lawes Resolutions*, 4; sig. A4ʳ.

[25] *Lawes Resolutions*, 118; Klein ed., *Daughters Wives and Widows*, 29.

> Time must play the Physitian, and I will helpe him a little: Why mourne you so, you that be widowes? Consider how long you have beene in subjection under the predeminance of parents, of your husbands, now you be free in libertie, and free… at your owne Law.[26]

For the first time in her life, a woman of property may gain personal autonomy and become financially independent in widowhood. We can choose whether these culturally and legally accurate observations are inclined to the sympathetic, the dispassionate, the ironic, or the mischievous—or any combination of them. While not necessarily mutually exclusive, they might indicate the need to be alert to whether compromises have been made between the law and entertainment and if so, of what kind.

Whether or not the tone is entirely serious, Prest is convinced that "the text is clearly not directed towards an exclusively female audience." In fact, crucially, he says that it is uncertain "that any women actually acquired or used the book." A book with the objective to *benefit* women was not necessarily written *for* women. The arguments of those promoting its proto-feminist credentials depend on an assumption of a relatively wider female readership—either actual or intended.[27] Various studies record the enormous growth of litigation in the decades around the turn of the seventeenth century, and agree that women constituted some 10–15% of litigants at common law.[28] The sheer numbers involved might well have suggested the women themselves, or the lawyers who represented them as a potential target audience.

Scripture is "the law's ultimate authority": the beginning of *The Lawes Resolutions* explains women's subordinate role to men in terms of the Biblical story of Adam and Eve—an approach, Klein points out, which has more in common with courtesy books for women than with legal compilations. However, within this hierarchical framework, she believes the author sees himself "as an advocate for women."[29] Similarly to Klein, Polito aligns the treatise with "conduct books and pamphlets produced by men for the

[26] *Lawes Resolutions*, 232.

[27] Prest, "Law and Women's Rights" 179, 181.

[28] See, for example, Stretton, *Women Waging Law*, 39–40. Stretton points out that in 1606, for example, given the scale of legal activity, even on a conservative estimate of 8%, some 8000 women were connected with actions on the central courts. Ibid., 42. For further information on levels of litigation, see, for example, Brooks, *Pettyfoggers and Vipers*; Erickson, *Women and Property*; Muldrew, *The Economy of Obligation*.

[29] Klein, *Daughters Wives and Widows*, 27–28 (28).

instruction of women."[30] Suzanne Hull lists *The Lawes Resolutions* in her "Basic List of Books *for* Women, 1475–1640" [my emphasis].[31] Stenton interprets the author's general expression of thanks to "woman kind" as evidence of his "assurance that women would read him."[32] Goodrich identifies the treatise's style as that of a "self-help" book. He explains that because the status of women was deemed "politically suspect" and "legally uncertain," the *querelle des femmes*, touching all aspects of the place and status of women, had been an increasingly troubling concern across Europe and was now emerging in law. *The Lawes Resolutions* represented an intervention in that debate. In that role, he is inclined to see the treatise in terms of "the defence of women…and the manipulation of hostile rules to the benefit of an oppressed class." His analysis acknowledges the playful ambiguity of the text. However, the location of the text within the scope of the *querelle des femmes* is more sustainable.[33]

Despite the technical nature of the treatise, Prest tells us that some of the "conceptual apparatus and terminology," particularly concerning land law, "however incomprehensible to modern readers, would have been more or less familiar to a great many women in the early seventeenth century." Nor, apparently, would they have been deterred by black letter typeface. On the other hand, since "some…Latin (notoriously less accessible to girls than to boys)" would have been essential, along with French, "as well as access to a fairly extensive law library," this seems to exclude easy reference for other than legal professionals. In addition, much of its contents concern statute law—much of which was obsolete by 1632—or it refers to recent, unreported judgments deriving from the "wholly masculine" didactic tradition of legal scholarship established in the medieval Inns of Court.[34]

If the style of *The Lawes Resolutions* does not identify a specific target audience, there might be clues in its manner of address. Klein notes that

[30] Polito, "Wit, Will and Governance," 24.

[31] Hull, *Chaste, Silent and Obedient*, 166. She defines the criteria for eligibility for inclusion in her list at ix-x: books are required to satisfy at least one category. *The Lawes Resolutions* would satisfy her first and third categories: 1. "Books specifically directed to women"—via title, preface, dedication, introduction, text and so on; and 3. "books with separate sections on women's duties or roles."

[32] Stenton, *The English Woman*, 61; *Lawes Resolutions*, 3.

[33] Goodrich, "Gynaetopia: Feminine Genealogies," 291, 279, 292.

[34] Prest, "Law and Women's Rights," 176, 182–83, 176, 177. Greenberg, *Legal Treatises*, xxxiv, while assuming a putative female readership, also suggests usage of the treatise to have been predominantly by legal professionals.

the author "addresses women usually in the third person but sometimes also in the first and second person," similarly to a lawyer addressing his clients. Polito infers that "the book, like its implied readers, is gendered female and is similarly in need of protection." She assumes the faux-modest epistle signifies an expectation that his "project…will be scorned," although it is more likely simply to be following the manner of publishing convention.[35] However, despite the claims it makes for its objective to serve women, Prest points to the author's concluding address to "those, that have but newly taken acquaintance of Littleton": in other words, students who were by definition, male. Unlike Klein, he finds the text only "occasionally" addresses a "putative female reader," and there is at least one instance in which the usually un-gendered reader "is revealingly addressed as 'Sir'," while on another, being directed "for *his* better instruction" [my emphasis] to Coke's *Commentary on Littleton*—the province of the legal professional. He finds these to be the only beneficiaries of the "antique obscurities and modern complexities, adopting the brusque style of the legal commonplace book or case report" indulged by *The Lawes Resolutions*.[36]

Nor is there more clarification to be found in the narrative text of the treatise: women are certainly represented as "legally underprivileged" and "vulnerable to exploitation," but any sympathy is necessarily reserved for women who have, or will inherit, property since it is with their affairs that *The Lawes Resolutions* is primarily concerned. Yet at the same time, Prest observes "the extent to which *The Lawes Resolutions* remains imprisoned within the traditional framework of inns of court learning" and their focus on the common law and ancient courts. As we have seen, there was a notable increase in common law litigation between 1560 and 1640, while the cultural preoccupation with property law was expressed in the parallel expansion in Chancery "and other conciliar jurisdictions." Women were apparently involved in some 16–17% of Chancery suits as "principal plaintiffs" in the second half of the sixteenth century, and from 1613 to 1714, up to 25%. In view of this emphasis, *The Lawes Resolutions* apparently fails

[35] Klein, *Daughters Wives and Widows*, 28; Polito, "Wit, Will and Governance," 26. See, for example, Anderson, "The Rhetoric of Paratext," 638, where he warns about the difficulty facing those who attempt to "navigate ironic paratexts."

[36] Prest, "Law and Women's Rights," 179; *Lawes Resolutions*, 403, 79, 276.

to meet the needs of the most legally active group of women—those seeking to protect their property interests.[37]

There is little dispute that the purpose of publishing in English, rather than the law French that was still customary for professional legal writings, was indeed to make the contents accessible to the lay reader. But Prest points out that what is known about literacy rates for women at the time suggest that its predominant readership must have been found among "the exclusively male membership of the inns of court."[38] And the need for accessibility existed at all levels of the law—it was not necessarily (if at all) equated with female learning—remembering, for instance, that all twenty editions of Dalton's *Country Justice* were printed in English.[39] In these circumstances, lack of access to appropriate education and knowledge, and relevance militate against a wide female readership of *The Lawes Resolutions.*

If women in any quantity are discounted, the questions still remain of whom and for what purpose the treatise was published. The lack of citation by commentators, of course, does not necessarily mean lack of use by students or practitioners at lower levels of the law. Possibly more significantly though, publication of *The Lawes Resolutions* coincided with a growing movement to impose some order on the "bulky and heterogeneous mass…which constituted the common law of early modern England." Like the inconsistent legal record-keeping of the period, it seems that documentation of the law was also fairly chaotic: "English legal literature effectively consisted of little more than collections of case reports, statutes and writs, arranged on a merely chronological or alphabetical basis." Recognition of this state of affairs led to a strong interest in "methodising the law…throughout the first half of the seventeenth century." The moves both to broaden the readership and to impose some methodology might have influenced publication, although the work still contains examples that comprise "a formidable barrage of legal

[37] Prest, "Law and Women's Rights," 179, 180, and 181–183 (181). Prest, 182, find a study which suggests that, in the reign of James, the percentage of women as principal plaintiffs in Chancery suits might have risen to as much as 40%.

[38] Ibid., 180–181 (181). But see also Hubbard, *Reading, Writing and Initialing*, 557, 567: she explores the "complicated hierarchy" of literacy skills that finds reading was learned before writing, and blackletter taught first. Her analysis of marks or signatures on church court depositions suggests that "at least a quarter of London women had at least begun learning how to read."

[39] Dalton, *The countrey justice* (1618).

authority…unglossed technical terms and untranslated Latin tags," which expand alongside the length and complexity of the matter under discussion.[40] However, the publishing world, like any other business, was driven by commercial considerations, and evidence for the decision to update and reproduce the work, might well lie outside the text itself: in the book trade.

Law Books and the Print Trade

Law books did not only find a market with legal professionals. The materiality of books and the culture of book buying, as well as their contents, contributed to their popularity. Some, such as bibles, prayer books and grammars, were commercial staples, but as well as responding to demand, printers and publishers had to anticipate, if not create, the market in order to make a profit and establish an enduring business.[41] The ambiguities of the presentation and title of *The Lawes Resolutions of Womens Rights* might then indicate a deliberate attempt to broaden its customer base.

From the mid-sixteenth century, and during the seventeenth, book ownership increasingly became a status symbol, often being listed among the effects of the deceased. The interest in books as a consumer product was accompanied by a rapid growth in the use of both public and private libraries, although there is little evidence to suggest women independently owned books to any extent.[42]

The physical form of a book inevitably has the capacity to influence the way it is perceived and read. Within the historically technical constraints of the materials, print conventions and the expectations of its readers contribute to those perceptions. Maureen Bell identifies how "author, compositor, printer, publisher, editor…buyer and reader…singly or collaboratively" influence "choices of paper, format, type, ornament, illustration, binding and page layout." In addition to these factors, an important consideration in relation to publication of *The Lawes Resolutions* is the assumed readership of legal practitioners.[43]

[40] Prest, "Law and Women's Rights," 180, 181, 176.

[41] On the economics of the book trade, and the market for profitable books, such as law books, see Lesser, *Renaissance Drama*, 26–51 esp. 26–38; Handover, *Printing in London*, 45–74.

[42] Leedham-Green and McKitterick, "Private and Public Libraries," esp., 323–26. On books and consumerism, see also Raven, *The Business of Books*, esp., 51–54.

[43] Bell, "*Mise-en-page*," 632.

The culture of commodification, and the rise of the gentry in Elizabethan England contributed to a correspondingly rapid increase in admissions to the Inns of Court. It endowed an element of "social cachet": even for those not seeking to pursue a legal career, some time spent at the Inns seemed to have provided an essential part of a gentleman's education. "In an extremely litigious society men of means had a ... need for a modicum of legal skill, which...would enable them better to cope with the suits of avaricious neighbours and troublesome tenants." The Inns were though, also regarded as the most direct and prestigious path to a professional career.[44] Law was also taught at Oxford and Cambridge, but the intake was generally from those lower in the social order, and the numbers greater. Those who trained at the Universities went on to practise civil law in the maritime and ecclesiastical courts and chancery, not common law.[45]

Legal education at the Inns comprised three main elements: "private reading, court attendance and participation in...aural learning exercises." Prest maintains that "even before the introduction of printing" reading was probably always the most important means of learning.[46] However, John Baker tells us that libraries at the Inns were "somewhat inadequate," and students were expected to create their own manuscript books by "borrowing and transcribing, common-placing, and collecting precedents."[47] There was a "proliferation" of law books in the sixteenth century, but no satisfactorily formalised relationship between printing and legal education meant many were of little benefit to the student—either being hugely detailed and multi-volumed or insufficiently comprehensive.[48]

Property was the main expertise of most common lawyers, for which Littleton's *Tenures*, and Perkins's *Profitable Booke* generally offered a sound introduction. Baker confirms that *Littleton* "was very much a student primer" and that "the most basic requirements for a law student going to London were some bedding and a Littleton." He also identifies Christopher St German's *Doctor and Student* as "useful," aimed at the

[44] Prest, "Legal Education," 21, 23, 20. Prest, 20, finds that the "total annual student intake [of the Inns of Court] never rose above two thirds that of either Oxford or Cambridge."

[45] Kimball, "Legal Education, Liberal Education," 198; see also Boon and Webb, "Legal Education and Training," 82–89.

[46] Prest, "Legal Education," 25.

[47] Baker, "English Law Books," 476.

[48] Prest "Legal Education," 24, 32.

student rather than the lawyer, and not so much a law book as a discussion "of selected legal principles."[49]

Other than property and land law, the only practical interest for the country gentleman would have been "the law administered by justices of the peace and manorial courts"—neither of which occupied the syllabus at the Inns. By the beginning of the seventeenth century, the layman's involvement was largely confined to these minor courts, and several comprehensive manuals, such as Dalton's *Country Justice*, were available to assist him.[50]

Possibly surprisingly, at the other end of the scale, access to the statutes had already been transformed during Henry VII's reign by the advent of the printing press, and all copies made after 1500 were printed, ensuring far greater reliability and consistency than that of manuscript texts. Although increasingly subsidiary to common law, they were essential texts for lawyers to consult in conjunction with the Year Books and Reports. Even more surprisingly, they were printed in English, allowing circulation to extend widely beyond the legal profession. More generally, until the 1650s, the mystique of the law was preserved from humanist aspirations for accessibility by publishing only "elementary books" in English, and "professional" texts in Latin and law French.[51]

Books, by the beginning of the seventeenth century, offered commercial opportunity in an increasingly trade-based economy. However, the English book trade was in a process of development, and operating under legal and institutional constraints. Lesser explains how, unlike other industries, it required high initial capital investment. Publishers—who might speculate on and finance a project—were obliged to protect their investment. The two main vehicles of protection were the Stationers' Company, which was controlled by publishers—whatever their trade—and oversaw rights to copy, and the royal patent which protected "entire classes of books, like lawbooks or primers." At around the year 1600, there was a transition in publishing—away from printers to booksellers. At the same time, there was an increase in the arrangement whereby a printer might

[49] Ibid., 35. Prest, note 54, finds some sixty editions of Littleton's *Tenures* were published between 1481 or 1482, and 1640. See also Baker, "Common Law," 412. After the first (1530) edition of St German's *Doctor and Student*, Baker, "Common Law," note 10, observes that there were a further nineteen editions printed in English before 1600; the earliest record in the *ESTC* is an updated 1554 [1556?] edition.

[50] Prest, "Legal Education," 36. On Dalton's *Country Justice*, see Chap. 2.

[51] Baker, "Common Law," 422–23, Ibid., "English Law Books," 478.

publish a book, but then consign it to a bookseller for wholesale distribution. Printers found publishing less economically viable and the function of publisher-booksellers and trade printers became more polarised.[52]

Printers could generally not sustain themselves as publishers by relying only on Company rights; they needed the additional benefit offered by lucrative royal patents. Crucially "the book trade as a whole…depended on successfully predicting and creating the desires of the early modern book-buyers." The successful publisher needed both drive and imagination, but he also needed capital and the courage to invest it.[53]

A spirit of "adventure" was an advantage to the early publishers who entertained the possibility of wealth as "bespoke publishing" gave way to more speculative printing through the sixteenth century.[54] Law books were regulated by royal patent creating a monopoly of their printing. They were generally large, expensive and sought-after, and there was a constant need to maintain stocks of traditional legal texts. The demand, together with their re-circulation value and the drive to produce new titles to supersede "old standards," all contributed to steep price-increases from the 1560s for the ensuing century. Despite the reliable market for law books, Baker suggests that its necessarily limited size might have justified their elevated price. Ownership of the patent was clearly a valuable asset, and the only limits that were set were that the printer could own no more than two presses, and would be "liable to punishment for corrupt printing." However, the limit on presses clearly diminished the potential for unfettered wealth.[55]

Publishing *The Lawes Resolutions*

Although John More owned the royal patent for law books at the time *The Lawes Resolutions* was printed, he was not a stationer. The motive for his involvement, therefore, is not immediately apparent. An obvious possibility, of course, is potential financial gain. But on the surface, this explanation appears inconsistent with his circumstances. More, and an author

[52] Lesser, *Renaissance Drama*, 27, 29–30 (p. 30). See also Handover, *Printing in London*, 53–54.

[53] See Lesser, *Renaissance Drama*, 31–32, (p. 35).

[54] Ibid., 34; Raven, *Business of Books*, 352.

[55] Lesser, *Renaissance Drama*, p. 50 note 77; Raven, *Business of Books*, 51; Baker, "English Law Books," 479.

friend, John Dickenson, had both held government appointments under Sir Ralph Winwood (appointed commissioner to The Hague in 1603, and Secretary of State in 1614). There is no suggestion that they were themselves other than solvent. However, after his death, Dickenson and More undertook to pay Winwood's posthumous debts. In pursuit of this project, they apparently engaged in various "business ventures" together. Both Dickenson and the late Winwood had had some involvement with writing and publishing, and it seems possible that the acquisition of the law patent presented an opportunity.[56] With no direct experience of printing or publishing, it is consistent with his assumed objectives that More reached an agreement by means of his arrangement to assign the law patent to Flesher, and so to achieve a predictable income from it.[57] When the patent was assigned, it included the right to print some seventy titles to which several new works were added, which, as we know, included *The Lawes Resolutions.*[58] It was therefore Flesher and his partners who were the publishers and printers of *The Lawes Resolutions.* They clearly set out to exploit their opportunities to the full—of which the lucrative law patent was a significant part of their prospects—but by no means the whole.

By 1635, the partnership controlled nine presses—"more than one fifth of the printing presses in London." However, the business practices of the three partners could be suspect.[59] No doubt because of their sometimes unconventional and invariably ruthless methods, Flesher and his partners, according to Lesser, became "remarkably prosperous." Handover adds some refreshing colour to their approach: he recognises the achievements of Flesher and co., and their "exceptional gifts, Young for ruthless economics, Flesher as a skilful negotiator." But neither skill nor quality, he tells us, apparently went into their printing: "they were brigands; they were locusts, and they were execrable printers without the least interest in presswork or typography." They apparently exploited their monopoly, their workforce and the quality of the material and layout of the books. In fact, Handover links their work to "the decline in English printing and typography during the seventeenth century." And yet, conversely, Plomer

[56] See, *Oxford Dictionary of National Biography*, s.v. "Dickenson, John (c. 1570–1635/6), author and government official" (by Gavin Alexander), esp. paragraphs 6, 10, and 2. https://doi.org/10.1093/ref:odnb/7601. Accessed 6 April 2021.

[57] Baker, "English Law Books," 483–84, gives details of the arrangement.

[58] Bennett, *English Books and Readers*, 119.

[59] Handover, *Printing in London*, 54; Blagden, *Stationers Company*, 139–40; Plomer, *Dictionary of the Booksellers*, 76.

refers to "the history of the best work of the trade in London" as "practically the history of three men"—Haviland, Flesher and Young. This was the environment surrounding the men finally responsible for publication of *The Lawes Resolutions.*[60]

Possibly three separate stages were involved in the production of the treatise: first, the original manuscript collected and drafted by the "dead" author, then the updating and editing and finally the investment in its publication by Flesher. At each stage, the decision is likely to have been motivated by a different balance of aims and considerations—although those of Flesher et al. might now be apparent. In the atmosphere of the print trade, several aspects of the treatise fit with what we know or can surmise about the commercial imperative: the anonymity of the author, the deliberate ambiguity of title page, the demand for a more structured and methodical legal canon, the decision to print in English for the lay reader.

Whether its black letter typeface was a pragmatic decision, or another commercial ploy to give *The Lawes Resolutions* greater authenticity—to attract either legal professionals or lay collectors—remains another mystery. Despite its association with low culture ("broadside ballads, chapbooks, romances"), according to Lesser, exceptionally, "almost all law books were printed in black letter." He suggests that we should "hesitate" before accepting the association of roman with higher, and black letter with lower culture.[61] Conversely, handbooks produced from the early seventeenth century for the lay reader, such as Dalton's *Country Justice*, are in roman typeface.[62]

However, whatever commercial tactics were employed, we also know that sales of *The Lawes Resolutions* did not justify a second edition. It was not used as an authority by the legal profession, and concentrated on outdated statute law; nor was it recommended for use by students at the Inns of Court. It did not address the most significant areas of legal concern for

[60] Lesser, *Renaissance Drama*, 32 note 22; Handover, *Printing in London*, 56–58; Plomer, *History of English Printing*, 170.

[61] Lesser, "Typographic Nostalgia," 99, 103–104 (p. 103). His chapter discusses black letter and roman print in a semiotic context: he suggests the typeface is a "signifier" rather than as a "simple index to readers" (p. 104).

[62] Dalton's *Country Justice* (1618), and all subsequent editions are printed in roman typeface as, for example, is *The Complete justice* ([London (?): n. pub.], 1637), and *A manuall or analecta* (1641) and their respective later editions to, as well as Horne's, *Mirror of Justices* (1646).

women, trusts and equitable settlements and litigation in Chancery. It is also likely that, of the few women who might have been able to read it, even fewer would have had access to the supporting material to enable its contents to be of practical use. Nor is there evidence of women having read it.

Its lack of functionality, together with the fact that *The Lawes Resolutions* still appears decades later in catalogues of legal works, suggests a project intended by its publishers to have as broad an appeal as possible, but which failed to meet the needs of any—other than those collecting books for their commodity interest, either as a status symbol or to establish a library. Those involved might have anticipated a broadening of legal and lay interest in more accessible works, and have perceived a genuine need to illuminate the subject of law as it affects women. However, the most comfortable place to situate the work is, as Goodrich assumes, within the *querelle de femmes*—adding weight to the commercial argument.

Lesser observes that: "Most scholars…are generally content to end their analysis of the motives behind publication with a vague claim that a text was popular at its time of printing." Such a claim clearly cannot be true in this instance. He argues that the dynamic which demanded the publisher anticipate the market contradicts such an assumption. Instead he suggests that the publisher had to make a judgment based on the text itself—a judgment, in the case of *The Lawes Resolutions*, that appears to have been wrong.[63]

Rape Law, Criticism and *The Lawes Resolutions*

Regardless of who wrote or read *The Lawes Resolutions* in its own time, the text as a source for the modern critic should be treated with caution. The treatise turns to rape in the final parts of the work. The problems it presents as a sole legal source lie as much in its presentation as its contents. Both style and layout contribute to the potential for confusion. (Several critical errors arose prior to its availability in roman type via *EEBO* circa 2007.) The author resorts to literary conceits and the recognisable stereotypes of classical and popular literature to illuminate an ostensibly legal manual, and so creates space for ambivalence and interpretation. When the treatise turns to discussion of the statutes, the layout means that the preamble, clauses, and commentary, fact and opinion, are difficult to

[63] Lesser, *Renaissance Drama*, 41.

distinguish. Some commentary is misleading. And, although large sections of the text reproduce the statutes, not all statutes are complete.

> Section 20 introduces the subject "Of Rape". It is set out below is in its entirety:
>
> Chuse now whether yee will imagine, that the widdow hath agreed with him which was her husbands bane, or that she hath pursued him to death: She remaineth from henceforth a widdow, giving her selfe to almes and deeds of charitie, and of this good minde are many of our widdowes, which purpose constantly to live out the residue of their dayes in a devout remembrance of their deare husbands departed, to whom perhaps they made vowes never to marrie againe after their deaths. But to what purpose is it for women to make vowes, when men have so many millions of wayes to make them break them? And when sweet words, faire promises, tempting, flattering, swearing, lying will not serve to beguile the poore soule: then with rough handling, violence, and plaine strength of armes, they are, or have beene heretofore, rather made prisoners to lusts theeves, than wives and companions to faithfull honest lovers: So drunken are men with their owne lusts, and the poyson of *Ovids* false precept,
>
> *Vim licet appellant, vis est ea grata puellis.* [They call force allowed, force is pleasing to girls].[64]
>
> That if the rampier of Lawes were not betwixt women and their harmes, I verily thinke none of them, being above twelve yeares of age, and under an hundred, being either faire or rich, should be able to escape ravishing.
>
> This is therefore a matter concerning maids, wives, widdowes, and women of all degrees and conditions, if either they be, or possesse anything worth the having, and because the ignorance of Law may here turne a mollifying heart to harme, I were to blame, if I left my Schollers without warning to take heed.[65]

Whatever the authorial point of view, and however tongue-in-cheek, these paragraphs are revealing of cultural interdependencies. They introduce ideas about gender stereotypes, the real and perceived balance of power in marriage, and how sexual relationships were understood and transacted, as well as alluding to the legal implications that follow from them. But, in doing so, they also bring rape within the comic narrative surrounding gender relations—a characteristic of the *querelle des femmes*—and they assume the reader's familiarity with Ovid. In this context, Goodrich

[64] Translation by Garrett, "Sexual Consent," 37.

[65] *Lawes Resolutions*, 376–77.

identifies the cultural difficulties with the concept of the feminine that "forced the law to mix with other literatures and to search the languages of theology, nature, philosophy, medicine, politics, ethics, and other occult sciences to find some way of characterising an essentially inessential being."[66] The author of *The Lawes Resolutions* employs ambiguity and humour to mediate between the law's theory and the actuality to which it might apply.

The extract begins with a vignette of ambiguous female morality; its style is apparently playful. It describes figures recognisable in literature. The seemingly virtuous widow and her indeterminable relationship with "him which was her husbands bane" might translate to the sexually voracious widow of city comedy infamy.[67] Then there are those chaste heroines who resist the "sweet words, faire promises, tempting, flattering, swearing, lying," as men attempt seduction, coercion and/or resistible force. They are contrasted to their signified opposites—the women who are besieged and may succumb, with more or less resistance, to the attentions of the men with their "million ways" (the abandoned maidens of ballad and complaint). Whether virtuous or resolute, or neither, women are characterised as "poore soule[s]"—probably of weak will and game for male attention. The language and meaning are imprecise, and the Neo-Classical, debate of life or honour, and the Christian proscription of suicide, are invoked by that very ambivalence.[68] The fulcrum on which the scale from virtue to seduction and/or rape balances is, of course, vulnerable to re-positioning. The tone and descriptive style encourage the ambiguity that critics find. But it might be argued that the author of *The Lawes Resolutions* simply recognises the complexity of human behaviours: women might be disadvantaged in law, but he does not pretend they are not without human weaknesses. Unfortunately, recognition of female frailty then, as today, muddies the objective view and definition of rape, to the detriment of the female victim.

But, having introduced the idea of female virtue vested in women by formulaic typecasting (and a prerequisite to a valid appeal of rape), the

[66] Goodrich, "Gynaetopia: Feminine Genealogies," 294.

[67] *OED Online*, s.v. "bane, n. 1," defines "bane" variously as 1. "murderer; one who causes the death, or destruction of another," 4. "…causes ruin, or is 'pernicious to well-being; the agent or instrument of ruin, or woe', the 'curse'." https://www.oed.com/view/Entry/15183?rskey=7UecUN&result=1. Accessed 6 April 2021.

[68] The debate generated by St Augustine's question of why, "if…chaste," the raped Lucretia of Roman mythology committed suicide. See St. Augustine, *the citie of God*, I. 18.

author of *The Lawes Resolutions* then turns to the nature of men. He describes men as "drunken...with their owne lusts, and the poyson of *Ovids* false precept." The prominence given to the precept suggests that the notion has familiar currency. This in turn implies a recognised tension between the implied "natural" impulse for men to assert their sexual desires and the social imperative for women to defend their chastity at all costs. The author alludes to the law in expressing his fear that unbridled male lust is such that without strict laws no females "being above twelve years of age, and under a hundred, being either fair or rich, should be able to escape ravishment." The ages introduce a mix of legal fact with humour, exploiting stereotypes familiar from life and drama: on the one hand, the age of consent, on the other, the implication that any woman up to the age of a hundred might be vulnerable to male lust.[69] Youth is associated with physical desirability and age with the opposite; but the older woman may, of course, be sufficiently rich and vulnerable to outweigh a man's reluctance.

In Section 21 of the treatise, "Ravishment in two sorts," the author continues to combine metaphor and moral outrage to give colour to his exposition. He again appropriates examples from literature to enliven his commentary. "Ovid's false precept" is now fleshed out into the figures of classical rape mythology: Lucrece, Helen and Paris, and the Sabine Women. Analogy might help to illuminate the laws of rape, elopement and abduction, but the resort to mythical characters reinforces cultural perceptions that elide boundaries between imaginary ideals of women and the temporal reality with which the law is required to deal. It also assumes a universal interpretation of the character and behaviours of mythical figures.

Most importantly though, the narrative style appears to have been a significant factor in modern critical attempts to seek significance in the alternative use of the words "rape" and "ravishment." The Section reads as follows:

> There are two kindes of Rape, of which though the one be called by the common people, and by the Law it selfe, Ravishment; yet in my conceit it borroweth the name *from rapere,* but unproperly, for it is no more but *Species stupri* [form of rape] a hideous hatefull kinde of whoredome in him which committeth it, when a woman is enforced violently to sustaine the

[69] Despite the controversy (see Chap. 3), the author of the treatise assumes that the age of consent remained twelve subsequent to the 1575–6 statute.

> furie of brutish concupiscence: but she is left where she is found, as in her owne house or bed, as *Lucrece* was, and not hurried away, as *Helen* by *Paris*, or as the Sabine women were by the Romans, for that is both by nature of the word, and definition of the matter: The second and right ravishment, *Cum quis leonestae famae foeminam, sive virgo, sive vidua, sive sanctimonialis sit inuitis illis in quorum est potestate, abducit. Neque refert, an quis (volente vel nolente rapta) id faciat, nam vis quae Parentibus vel Curatoribus sit, maxime spectat.* [The passage describes the taking away of a wife, virgin, widow or nun, with or against her will, from the authority of her family or guardian. It is not a direct quote from any one statute].[70] It seemeth the first kinde of rape deserved alwayes death by Gods Lawes, unlesse the woman ravished were unbetrothed, so that the ravisher might marrie her, as you may read *Deuteronomy, chap. 22. vers. 23.* and by the Civill Law. *Raptores,* in the second kinde, *subjiciebantur poenae mortis rapta si fuent ingenua* [were subject to the penalty of death if kidnapping were of one of nobility]. How hainous they bee both, and have a long time beene, by the Lawes of England, yee shall now perceive.[71]

In the first sentence, the author acknowledges the interchangeable, common and legal usage of the term "ravishment," before expressing his personal, moral concern at its euphemistic representation of such "a hideous hatefull" act. This paragraph has been a focus for modern critics attempting to clarify and interpret the semantic and legal muddle associated with the terminology of rape and ravishment. But, as discussed in Chaps. 2 and 3, it has defied definitive consensus throughout history. In her essay, "The First Captive: The Kidnapping of Pocahontas," Karen Robertson does recognise the inconsistency in sixteenth-century usage of the terms 'rape' and 'ravishment', but is also led by *The Lawes Resolutions* to engage in the discussion about definitions, confusing the author's frustration at the inadequacy of the word 'ravishment' and his unsuccessful attempt at legal clarification.

Other comments are careless such as when, in section 21 above, referring to rape (as opposed to abduction), the author cites marriage via "Deuteronomy, chap. 22 verse 23 and by the Civil Law" as an alternative

[70] Robertson, "The First Captive," 86, translates the passage as follows: "When anyone carries off a woman of good fame, either an unmarried maid, a widow, or a religious woman, against the will of those to whom that power [authority] belongs. Nor is it allowed (whether she is willing or unwilling that he do this) for the violent act which occurs belongs to the kin or guardians."

[71] *Lawes Resolutions*, 377–78.

to death for rape of an unmarried woman. The notion of marriage to the rapist had become a legal impossibility under Westminster II (1285), with the crime decreed a felony, and the prohibition of "consent after."[72] Again, this invites a potential error on the part of anyone relying on the treatise for their understanding of early modern law, leading to the notion that marriage to the rapist was still a legally sanctioned practice (rather than a pragmatic or useful device for dramatists). Robertson, for example, identifies it as "extraordinary provisions of English rape law in the early seventeenth century," identifying it as evidence of the law's priority of property over the woman's ordeal.[73]

After the author's introductory commentary on Sections 20 and 21, *The Lawes Resolutions* moves on to provide a summary first of ancient, then statute law. However, the reader has first to separate comment and opinion from law, and be alert to any truncation of the relevant statutes. It discusses both sequences, sub-divided by statute, in simple chronological order under the undifferentiating main heading of "Rape," without any distinction between rape and abduction statutes. However, at the end of his commentary on Richard II's closing of the loophole of "consent after" and marriage to the rapist, the author introduces a final paragraph by saying: "And now cometh the second rape by abduction." He condemns "avarice" as being "as great an agent as carnality," expressing disgust that "now men turned themselves for loves sake into Centaures first, and tooke on them the shape of Buls afterward." However the legal significance is easily overlooked amongst the vivid narrative before the text moves to the next section—Henry VI's 1453 statute to void bonds made by women under duress. The author misleadingly identifies this as the first statute concerned with abduction, without any explanation of the significance.[74] The statutes then continue to be presented in a single chronological order. Coke, for instance, addresses the two crimes under the separate headings of "Rape" and "Felony for carrying away a Woman against her

[72] See Chap. 3.

[73] Robertson, "First Captive," 84–89 (p. 85), citing *Lawes Resolutions*, 377–78.

[74] *Lawes Resolutions*, 383; *Statutes of the Realm*, II, 367, 31 Henry VI c. ix, 1453. The statute does indeed envisage that such women might be abducted or tricked away from their families, and forced to marry "against their owne liking." But it does not allude to sexual violation (which, in modern terms, we might assume by definition): it remains at the purely transactional level of redressing the financial loss signed away "by Obligations." See Ives, "'Agaynst taking'," 23–24.

Will, &c"—that is, abduction.[75] Under his interpretation, their meaning is founded on the assumptions and dependencies created by understanding and reading them in their correct sequence. For critics relying on *The Lawes Resolutions* alone, this is not necessarily obvious.

Throughout the treatise, commentary can appear either superficial or mischievous. For example, the author dismisses Henry VI's 1453 statute as "too meek and gentle, something like him that made it," without analysis, before then introducing Henry VII's 1487 abduction act as "a better complaint." Ives notes that it is the latter, rather than the former, which is legally superfluous. In fact, without any supporting rationale, the comment might pass as a mischievous aside (possibly, even, privileging Shakespeare's literary view of Henry VI over legal analysis).[76]

Two of the three most common misapprehensions the treatise allows are those that equate ravishment with abduction, and the belief that there remained a provision for rape to be abated by marriage to the perpetrator. The third is a more subtle inference that *The Lawes Resolutions* is an established source of legal authority. But a failure to distinguish authorial comment from legal framework can lead to mistaken assumptions about the status of its contents. It must be, at least in part, because this misperception holds sway that the work is "ubiquitous" in modern criticism. However, while Barbara Baines assumes that *The Lawes Resolutions* carries legal authority, she also notes the lack of professional interest in it at the time, and is sceptical about the extent of both its professional and female readership, perceiving its advice to women as "patronizing."[77]

But errors arising from lack of clarity in the presentation of the treatise can disrupt the entire basis of an argument. In her essay, and later chapter, on Helen of Troy, Laurie Maguire appears to mistake the medieval and early modern legal definitions of and the notion of 'consent after' and elopement (a property crime), with a modern notion of adultery. Unfortunately her argument depends on an assertion that *The Lawes Resolutions* classifies ***adultery*** [my emphasis] as rape and devotes a section to it. The word "adultery" appears nowhere in the twenty-seven page section concerned with rape, while sexual infidelity within marriage was a

[75] Coke, *The Third Part*, 60–62. See also Ives, "'Agaynst taking awaye'," 22–24, and Sokol and Sokol, *Shakespeare Law and Marriage*, 109; like Coke, they each identify the Henry VII 1487 act as the first abduction act.

[76] Ives, "Agaynst taking awaye," 24–25.

[77] Baines, *Representing*, 64–70, 82 note 26. At 81, note 19, Baines also points out Bashar's puzzling bibliographic attribution of *The Lawes Resolutions* to "Nicholas Brady."

matter for the church courts.[78] Unfortunately Maguire also commends Carolyn Sale's account of consent in the context of Lavinia's rape in *Titus Andronicus.*[79] Among a number of errors, an element of Sale's confusion appears to arise from the historic syntax of *The Lawes Resolutions.* Her ostensibly knowledgeable exposition of how the laws of rape and abduction were deployed and applied by and against women also assumes the treatise has professional authority. Alongside legal reports, examples from the treatise combine its misleading representation of the statutes with her own to undermine the overall argument. For instance, while suggesting that *The Lawes Resolutions* identifies a direct link between a progressive weakening in rape law and the notion of consent, she finds that the treatise cites the ancient law of Athelstan as "precipitat[ing] the devolution of the crime into a 'verie small trespasse'."[80] But *The Lawes Resolutions* actually reveals the precise opposite:

> Was it *Mag. Chart. cap. 29.* Or what was it that made the Law so meeke in *Edward* the first his time that the first Statute against Rape, speaketh of it so mildly, *as if it had beene* [my emphasis] at Common Law a verie small trespasse.[81]

Nor at any point does *The Lawes Resolutions* attribute significance to the word 'consent'. It simply reprises the ancient laws, of which Athelstan's is the earliest recorded version.[82] The passage identifies Westminster I as responsible for reducing the capital penalty to two years' imprisonment and a fine. Although this might be a controversial reading of the statutes (see Chap. 3), the restitution of 'life and member' ten years later by Westminster II, and the statutory death penalty that remained extant, and was reinforced in Elizabeth's 1575–6 statute, are incompatible with the notion of a progressive weakening of the law (see Chap. 3).

[78] Maguire, "Helen of Troy," 39; ibid., *From Homer to Hollywood*, 99–100. The error appears to derive from Jocelyn Catty, *Writing Rape, Writing Women in Early Modern England: Unbridled Speech* (1999) 13, whom Maguire cites, and from misinterpretation of *Lawes Resolutions*, 390.

[79] Maguire, *From Homer to Hollywood*, 221, note 16; Sale, "Representing Lavinia," 1–27.

[80] Sale, "Representing Lavinia," 5. Sale follows *The Lawes Resolutions* in using the variant "Adelstan." As we have seen from Chap. 2, loss of eyes and members was the penalty prior to Westminster I, and life and members in Athelstan's time.

[81] *Lawes Resolutions*, 380. *The boke of Magna Carta* (London: Redman, 1534), chapter 29, fol. 7, sets out the right of habeas corpus.

[82] On the ancient law, see *Bracton*, II, 418; on the question of consent, see Chap. 2.

Neither is William the Conqueror's injunction against capital punishment "for *any* transgression" [my emphasis] necessarily directed solely to rape.[83] Nor is Westminster I's provision for "'*any* damsel within age'" (Sale's emphasis) evidence of the law's inclusiveness: it specifically defines underage girls for whom sex was statutory rape under any circumstances. The foregoing inevitably leads to misinterpretation of the subsequent statutes.[84] These examples show the pitfalls associated with reading both *The Lawes Resolutions* and the statutes themselves. It is only fair to emphasise that there are many instances of critical error arising from the assumption that *The Lawes Resolutions* is an authoritative representation of the written law. But the foregoing not only demonstrates how readily errors can be accepted, broadcast and inextricably compounded, but they also reinforce the need to be alert to the status of source documents and to consider the statutes in their full sequences.

It is consistent with the anomalous nature of *The Lawes Resolutions* that, in its own time, its readership was limited, while a wider audience has seemingly been found among modern critics. Scrutiny in the context of ancient law, the statutes and contemporary treatises makes clearer how and why, in isolation, the treatise is an unreliable source. Once the reader is alert to the ambiguity of *The Lawes Resolutions*, the uncertain status of the treatise can be identified through its language, voice and tone; its format and type face are not compatible with other works of supposedly similar type, nor did it achieve the repeated editions that more successful works enjoyed. Particularly telling is that neither early modern legal professionals, nor modern legal historians, cite the work when discussing rape law or legal works. It appears nowhere in the references of, for example Baker, Ives or J.B. Post. And those who have investigated its origins and purpose, such as Goodrich and Prest, have done so with a view to the exploration of an anomaly.[85]

Despite its capacity to mislead, it is important to keep in mind how useful *The Lawes Resolutions* can be. It has a strong claim as a piece of social history, both as an object, and for its contribution to the *querelle de femmes*. It is a very useful source as an indicator and a starting point for

[83] Sale, "Representing Lavinia," 5; *Lawes Resolutions*, 379.

[84] Sale, "Representing Lavinia," 5, 6–8; *Statutes of the Realm*, I, 29, 3 Edward I, the First Statute of Westminster, c. xiii, 1275; Ibid., 87, 13 Edward I, the Second Statute of Westminster, c. xxxiv–xxxv, 1285.

[85] Post, "Ravishment of Women," 150–164.

legal enquiry, but it can only fulfil its potential value in conjunction with other material: statutes, commentary, case reports and robust analysis by legal historians. In his assessment of the likelihood that women read or were able to make use of the work, we should bear in mind Prest's comment that in order to do so they would need the basics of Latin, as well as French, and "access to a fairly extensive law library." What was a true principal for those approaching the text in early modern times, is also true today. If modern critics wish to cite *The Lawes Resolutions* in a legal context with confidence, they must also seek the validation of reliable supporting material.

Bibliography

Anderson, Randall, J. "The Rhetoric of Paratext in Early Printed Books". In *The Cambridge History of the Book: Vol. 4, 1557–1695*, edited by Barnard, and McKenzie. 2002.

Augustine. *Of the citie of God*. London: Eld, 1610.

Baker, J. H. "The Books of the Common Law", in *The Cambridge History of the Book in Britain: Vol. 3, 1400–1557*, edited by Lotte Hellinga, and J.B. Trapp. Cambridge: Cambridge University Press, 1999.

———. "English Law Books and Legal Publishing", in *The Cambridge History of the Book: Vol. 4, 1557–1695*, edited by Barnard, and McKenzie. 2002.

Barnard, John, and D. F. McKenzie, with the assistance of Maureen Bell, eds. *The Cambridge History of the Book in Britain: Vol. 4, 1557–1695.* Cambridge: Cambridge University Press, 2002.

Bell, Maureen. "*Mise-en-page*, Illustration, Expressive Form", in *The Cambridge History of the Book : Vol. 4, 1557–1695*, edited by Barnard, and McKenzie. 2002.

Bennett, H. S. *English Books and Readers, 1603 to 1640: Being a Study in the History of the Book Trade in the Reigns of James I and Charles I.* Cambridge: Cambridge University Press, 1970.

Blagden, Cyprian. *The Stationers' Company: a History, 1403–1959.* London: Allen and Unwin, 1960.

Boke of Magna Carta, The. London: Redman, 1534.

Boon, Andrew and Julian Webb. "Legal Education and Training in England and Wales: Back to the Future?", *Journal of Legal Education*, 58 (2008), 79–121.

Bracton, Henricus de. *De Legibus et Consuetudinibus Angliae. Bracton*, edited by George E. Woodbine, translated by Samuel E. Thorne, 4 vols. Cambridge, Mass.: Harvard University Press, 1968–77. II (1968).

Brooks, Christopher. *Pettyfoggers and Vipers of the Commonwealth: The 'Lower Branch' of the Legal Profession in Early Modern England.* Cambridge: Cambridge University Press 1986.

Brydall, John. *Privilegia magnatum apud Anglos.* London: Sawbridge, 1704.

Cannon, Christopher. "The Rights of Medieval English Women: Crime and the Issue of Representation", in *Medieval Crime and Social Control*, edited by Barbara A. Hanawalt, and David Wallace. London: University of Minnesota Press, 1998.

Catty, Jocelyn. *Writing Rape, Writing Women in Early Modern England: Unbridled Speech.* 1999. Revised reprint, Basingstoke: Macmillan, 2011.

Coke, Edward. *Institutes of the Laws of England*, 4 vols. New York and London: Garland, 1979.

—— *The Third Part of the Institutes of the Laws of England*, 4th edition. London: Brooke, 1797.

The Complete justice. [London (?): n. pub.], 1637.

Dalton, Michael. *The countrey justice containing the practice of the justices of the peace out of their sessions.* London: Islip, 1618.

E[dgar] T[homas]. *The Lawes Resolutions of Womens Rights: Or, The Lawes Provision for Woemen.* London: More, 1632.

Edgar, Thomas. *Two Charges.* London: Walbancke [1649, i.e. 1650].

Erickson, Amy. *Women and Property in Early Modern England.* London: Routledge, 1993.

Goodrich, Peter. "Gynaetopia: Feminine Genealogies of Common Law", *Journal of Law and Society*, 20 (1993): 276–308.

Greenberg, Lynne A. editor, *Legal Treatises, Early Modern Englishwoman*, Series 3: Essential Works for the Study of Early Modern Women, Part 1, vols 1–3, edited by Betty S. Travitsky and Anne Lake Prescott. Aldershot: Ashgate, 2005.

Halkett, Samuel, and John Laing. *A Dictionary of Anonymous and Pseudonymous Publications in the English Language 1475–1640*, edited by John Horden. Harlow: Longman, 1980.

Handover, P. M. *Printing in London from 1476 to Modern Times: Competitive Practice and Technical Invention in the Trade of Book and Bible Printing, Periodical Production, Jobbing etc..* London: Allen and Unwin, 1960.

Horne, Andrew. *The booke called the mirrour of justices.* London: Walbancke, 1646.

Hubbard, Eleanor. "Reading, Writing, and Initialing: Female Literacy in Early Modern London", *Journal of British Studies*, 54.3 (2015): 553–577.

Hull, Suzanne W. *Chaste, Silent and Obedient: English Books for Women 1475–1640.* San Marino: Huntington Library, 1982.

Ives, E. W. "'Agaynst taking awaye of Women': The Inception and Operation of the Abduction Act of 1487", in *Wealth and Power in Tudor England: Essays Presented to S.T. Bindoff*, edited by E. W. Ives, R.J. Knecht and J.J. Scarisbrick. London: Athlone Press, 1978: 21–44.

Kimball, Bruce A. "Legal Education, Liberal Education, and the Trivial Artes", *Journal of General Education*, 38 (1986): 182–210.

Klein, Joan Larsen. editor, *Daughters Wives and Widows: Writings by Men About Women and Marriage in England, 1500–1640*. Chicago: University of Illinois Press, 1992.

Leedham-Green, Elisabeth, and David McKitterick. "Ownership: Private and Public Libraries", in *The Cambridge History of the Book in Britain: Vol. 4, 1557–1695*, edited by John Barnard, and D.F. McKenzie, with the assistance of Maureen Bell, 6 vols. Cambridge: Cambridge University Press, 1999–2012, IV, 2002.

Lesser, Zachary. *Renaissance Drama and the Politics of Publication: Readings in the English Book Trade*. Cambridge: Cambridge University Press, 2004.

—— "Typographic Nostalgia: Play-Reading, Popularity, and the Meaning of Black Letter", in *The Book of the Play: Playwrights, Stationers, and Readers in Early Modern England*, edited by Marta Straznicky. Amherst and Boston: University of Massachusetts Press, 2006.

London, William. *A Catalogue of The Most Vendible Books in England*. London: [n. pub.], 1657.

Maguire, Laurie. *Helen of Troy: From Homer to Hollywood*. Chichester: Wiley-Blackwell, 2009.

—— "Helen of Troy: Representing Absolute Beauty in Language", *Sederi*, 16 (2006): 31–51.

Manuall or analecta… A, formerly styled The complete justice. London: Flesher, 1641.

Muldrew, Craig. *The Economy of Obligation: The Culture of Credit and Social Relations in Early Modern England*. Basingstoke: Macmillan, 1998.

Perkins, John. *A profitable booke of Maister John Perkins felowe of the inner temple treating the lawes of Englande*. London: Tottell, 1555.

Plomer, Henry R. *A Dictionary of the Booksellers and Printers Who Were at Work in England, Scotland and Ireland from 1641 to 1667*. London: Bibliographical Society, 1907.

—— *A Short History of English Printing 1476–1898*. London: Kegan Paul, Trench Trubner and Company, 1900.

Polito, Mary. "Wit, Will and Governance in Early Modern Legal Literature", *Mosaic*, 27. (1994): 15–34

Post, J. B., "Ravishment of Women and the Statutes of Westminster", in *Legal Records and the Historian: Papers Presented to the Cambridge Legal History Conference, 7–10 July 1975*, edited by J. H. Baker. London: Royal Historical Society, 1978.

Prest, Wilfred. "Law and Women's Rights in Early Modern England", *Seventeenth Century*, 6 (1991): 169–87

—— "Legal Education of the Gentry at the Inns of Court, 1560–1640", *Past and Present*, 38 (1967): 20–39.

Raven, James. *The Business of Books: Booksellers and the English Book Trade, 1450–1850*. London: Yale University Press, 2007.

Robertson, Karen. "The First Captive: The Kidnapping of Pocahontas", in *Women, Violence, and English Renaissance Literature: Essays Honoring Paul Jorgensen*, edited by Linda Woodbridge, and Sharon Beehler. Tempe: Arizona Center for Medieval and Renaissance Studies, 2003.

Saint German, Christopher. *The dyaloges in Englishe, betweene a doctour of divinitie, and a student in the lawes of Englande, newely corrected and imprinted wyth new addicions*. [London: Tottel, 1554 [1556?]].

Sale, Carolyn. "Representing Lavinia: The. In significance of Women's Consent in Legal Discourses of Rape and Ravishment and Shakespeare's *Titus Andronicus*", in *Women, Violence, and English Renaissance Literature: Essays Honoring Paul Jorgensen*, edited by Linda Woodbridge and Sharon Beehler. Tempe: Arizona Center for Medieval and Renaissance Studies, 2003.

Sheppard, William. *The touch-stone of common assurances, Or, A plain and familiar treatise opening the learning of the common assurances or conveyances of the kingdom*. London: M. F., 1648.

Sokol, B. J., and Mary. *Shakespeare, Law, and Marriage*. Cambridge: Cambridge University Press, 2003.

Statutes of the Realm, 12 vols. London: England Record Commission, 1810–1828.

Stenton, Doris Mary. *The English Woman in History*. New York: Schocken Books, 1977.

Stretton, Tim. *Women Waging Law in Elizabethan England*. Cambridge: Cambridge University Press, 1998.

Worrall, John. *Bibliotheca legume*. London: Worral, 1732.

CHAPTER 5

Conclusion

Abstract Both facts and the context surrounding the subject of rape in early modern England have been either overlooked or misrepresented in criticism for decades. This concluding chapter is a reminder of the legal and historical considerations crucial to informed discussion of rape in the early modern period, and of the important work of specialists in the field of law and history. More interesting opportunities for research emerge when rape is placed among the legal, political, social and cultural complexities that define any period of history.

Keywords Rape • Homicide

Rape is a horrific, sensational, dramatic crime: a fascinating topic with potential for investigation across the humanities. It is therefore surprising that discussion of the subject in the context of legal history has become moribund, and left in a state of misinformation and confusion. While detailed work by legal and social historians continues, across the wider academy rape is a subject that seems still to be haunted by the anachronistic ideology of the 1970s and 1980s that placed rape in a transhistorical continuum of misogyny and male oppression and left no space for enquiry into the complexities of history.

H. Barker, *Rape in Early Modern England*,
https://doi.org/10.1007/978-3-030-82609-3_5

If behaviour is timeless, history has nothing to teach us. Susan Brownmiller's 1975 insistence on rape as a transhistorical mechanism, by which men use violence to exert control over women, became an established starting point for the discussion of rape. The ideology of sexual violence as intrinsic to the structures of male authority was perpetuated by Nazife Bashar. She claimed that rape was a crime little prosecuted by male authorities because they were reluctant to hang a man for the violation of a woman. It was a debate in which Roy Porter, on the other hand, found that male authority was so deeply entrenched in traditional society that rape as a mechanism of control was irrelevant: his work indicated the complexity of the subject, and various circumstances that might impact behaviour and crime rates. But the polarised position of male oppression and victimhood had taken hold and provided a simple access point for critics across the academy. Unfortunately, it also not only closed down exploration of more interesting complexity, but also allowed misinformation to take hold. As literary critics took up Bashar as the unquestioned—if not unquestionable—authority, so subsequent critics followed in their footsteps. Instead of enrichment, dilution followed and misinformation spread and became commonplace.

In the meantime, historians Bernard Capp and Laura Gowing's work among the church court records finds that members of early modern communities were watchful of one another's moral behaviour: the late age of first marriages, the financial consequences of unwanted pregnancies and the importance of personal reputation made a society alert to the activities of their neighbours—and women played a prominent role in monitoring activities. Court records indicate men who forced themselves on their maidservants were seeking sex—albeit often with a sense of entitlement—rather than control. The men also understood that the risks to women in complaining made it likely they would get away with it. A woman's reputation could be ruined by acknowledging sexual activity outside marriage (even if forced), but if unsuccessful, she risked being the subject of defamation proceedings as well. However, Garthine Walker finds seventeenth-century newspaper reports of rape trials reveal often grotesque violence perpetrated against the victim. But, even if a rape prosecution failed, courts were looking for other charges to bring against the perpetrator. Society was confronted with the question that Walker raises: was the rapist "Everyman, or a Monster": is the potential to rape latent in all men, or is the rapist an aberrant? Investigation of interplay between the knowledge, perceptions and interests of society at a particular time in history and the effect of social conditions on the individual are far more interesting than monolithic and reductive paradigms that close down enquiry.

Nor can the extraordinarily low conviction rates for rape be co-opted to a simple model of misogyny. Ancient common law, medieval and early modern statutes and the pronouncements of individual judges and lawyers made clear their abhorrence at the crime. Despite the confusion and ambiguities arising from the statutes, rape remained a crime at common law throughout, and the punishments and penalties severe. Critics have taken issue not with what the law said, but what it did—or did not do. If challenging the low number of indictments, it must be remembered that the risk to the reputation of a woman who had been raped was considerable, even if the prosecution was successful. If she was to pursue the case, conviction rightly depended on evidence and standards of proof. While the requirements of the courts in the case of rape were common to many crimes and all felonies, rape carried the enduring challenge of being committed in a private place, usually devoid of witnesses. A woman might raise a hue and cry and call on those who would attest to her wounds and torn clothing, but ultimately the case would rest on a woman's word against a man's. The victim would be conscious of both these factors and those of the public shame and potential for being sued for defamation. Not only was it likely that a male judge and jury would be reluctant to convict a man simply on a woman's word, but in the case of rape, the penalty was death. Pronouncements by judges demonstrate their understandable caution in applying the death penalty for any crime. K.J. Kesselring's research indicates that there was, indeed, similar reluctance to hang a man for homicide. It may, then be less appropriate to berate historic law-makers, than to recognise the multiple complexities rape embodied. It is obvious that a woman's inferior social and moral status—particularly if of lower social standing—and the emphasis on her reputation, militated against making a rape appeal, and then in it succeeding. But the rules of evidence and the anxiety among judges about hanging an innocent man—both reasonable concerns—also played an essential part.

Gradually, changes in statute law meant it became more difficult to avoid punishment for rape. Sanctuary, pardons and benefit of clergy (claimed by recital of a verse from the Bible) were limited or removed in the late fifteenth and early sixteenth centuries. Although the rape statutes remained substantially unamended from the end of the sixteenth into the nineteenth century, knowledge progressed so that conception was no longer regarded as proof of consent. But in the courts over the eighteenth century, the introduction of the defence barrister—which might generally be regarded as a positive development—in the case of rape also introduced the culture of victim-blaming that remains a barrier for women bringing and succeeding with prosecutions today.

For literary scholars, in particular, past confusion offers grounds to revisit, compare and consider new readings. The contents of this book might provide some support for such an endeavour, but come with a consistent warning throughout: early modern rape law is not definitive, it has to be read in the knowledge and context of its contradictions, ambiguities and ongoing debates. The purpose has been to indicate what those might be, and where more specialist knowledge might be found. When experts in the field like J.B Post, Henry Ansgar Kelly and Caroline Dunn are unable to offer a unanimous, definitive interpretation of the medieval statutes, and of the various forms of the words 'rape' and 'ravishment', it is unwise for the non-specialist to make simple assumptions about the interpretation or intention of the law at any particular time. It is the specialists in the fields of law and history who can offer the knowledge to enrich the work of scholars across the academy. Their work might also be an essential reminder of the need to be historically specific: we might make comparisons and draw lessons, but it is anachronistic, if not arrogant, to judge the past from our position in the present. The situation in relation to rape prosecution and conviction today does not suggest we are in any way superior to our predecessors, nor does it suggest we are not. Rape presents an enduring problem whose cause and solutions lie in their own historical time.

Index[1]

[1] Note: Page numbers followed by 'n' refer to notes.

H. Barker, *Rape in Early Modern England*,
https://doi.org/10.1007/978-3-030-82609-3

FSC
www.fsc.org
MIX
Papier | Fördert gute Waldnutzung
FSC® C083411

Kolibri 360 GmbH
Ferdinand-Jühlke-Straße 7
99095 Erfurt, Deutschland
produktsicherheit@kolibri360.de